I0126120

Shaping the Future of Regulators

THE IMPACT OF EMERGING TECHNOLOGIES ON ECONOMIC REGULATORS

OECD

BETTER POLICIES FOR BETTER LIVES

This document, as well as any data and map included herein, are without prejudice to the status of or sovereignty over any territory, to the delimitation of international frontiers and boundaries and to the name of any territory, city or area.

The statistical data for Israel are supplied by and under the responsibility of the relevant Israeli authorities. The use of such data by the OECD is without prejudice to the status of the Golan Heights, East Jerusalem and Israeli settlements in the West Bank under the terms of international law.

Please cite this publication as:
OECD (2020), *Shaping the Future of Regulators: The Impact of Emerging Technologies on Economic Regulators*, The Governance of Regulators, OECD Publishing, Paris, *https://doi.org/10.1787/db481aa3-en*.

ISBN 978-92-64-49248-6 (print)
ISBN 978-92-64-62273-9 (pdf)

The Governance of Regulators
ISSN 2415-1432 (print)
ISSN 2415-1440 (online)

Foreword

Regulators are in a unique position, at the forefront of interaction with consumers, business, and government, and with direct oversight of markets that deliver essential services to citizens and the economy. They are characterised by technical expertise and organisational agility, making them essential players of the regulatory and policy ecosystems. This role is enhanced in a context subject to fast transformation, led by emerging technologies such as artificial intelligence, blockchain, machine learning, and big data analysis, that disrupt traditional business models and create new ways for consumers to interact with the providers of goods and services. Regulators have their fingers on the pulse of the markets and these transformative innovations.

Economic regulators are entrusted with a number of responsibilities that vary across jurisdictions and sectors. They often include ensuring that markets run efficiently and that consumers have access to good-quality services, as well as upholding competition and creating a level playing field for market actors. In the context of emerging technologies, regulators have to provide frameworks that foster innovation on the one hand and that continue to uphold these goals on the other. As such, the transformative effect of emerging technologies is deeply impacting the work of regulators and in some cases, calls into question whether the objectives, resources and tools of regulatory authorities are still fit for purpose.

In this context, this report showcases initiatives designed by regulators across sectors of the economy to get ahead of the curve in addressing some of these challenges and changes. The case studies presented in the report illustrate exercises as diverse as review of the stock of regulations, internal re-organisation, assessment of the regulator's resourcing levels, and the development of foresight capacity. They also bring to light how emerging technologies have had a positive impact on the way regulators design their regulatory and enforcement activities, for instance using live data and data driven regulation. In all of these areas, the need for enhanced co-operation (across sectors or national frontiers) and change management internally for a forward looking culture and staff keen on embracing new ways of working come to the fore.

The preparation of the report was prompted by discussions at the 12th meeting of the OECD Network of Economic Regulators in April 2019. The report marks the continuation, rather than the conclusion, of these discussions. As markets continue to change and as economies react to systemic shocks such as the COVID-19 pandemic, the need for agility and flexibility, as well as capacity for self-assessment by regulators remain essential. This report is a contribution to this important conversation and forms part of OECD work in the area of innovation, emerging technologies and regulation.

This report is part of the OECD work programme on the governance of regulators and regulatory policy, led by the OECD Network of Economic Regulators and the OECD Regulatory Policy Committee, with the support of the Regulatory Policy Division of the OECD Directorate of Public Governance. The Directorate's mission is to help government at all levels design and implement strategic, evidence-based and innovative policies that support sustainable economic and social development.

The report was presented to the OECD Network of Economic Regulators and the Regulatory Policy Committee for approval in October 2020 by written procedure.

Acknowledgments

The report was co-ordinated by Anna Pietikainen and drafted by Miguel Amaral, Claire Leger, Anna Pietikainen and Ana Simion. The work benefited from the direction and support of Elsa Pilichowski, Director, and János Bertók, Deputy Director, OECD Public Governance Directorate and Nick Malyshev, Head of the Regulatory Policy Division, Public Governance Directorate. Early versions of the case studies were assembled by Miguel Amaral, Lorenzo Casullo, James Drummond, Andrea Perez, and Anna Pietikainen. Jennifer Stein and Ciara Muller edited and prepared the report for publication, and editorial support was provided by Andrea Uhrhammer. Comments were provided by Jacob Rivera Perez, Barbara Ubaldi, Gregor Virant, and Benjamin Welby.

The case studies presented in the report were first prepared for discussion at the 12th meeting of the Network of Economic Regulators (NER) in April 2019 on whether regulators' legal frameworks and attributes (mandate, powers, functions) and management capacities (resources, technical capacity, agility) are adequate in a context of market transformation and disruptive technologies, and how regulators are using new technologies to design better regulatory tools, processes and services.

The Secretariat would like to thank to all contributors to the case studies without whom the discussions at the NER meeting and this report would not have been possible: Baethan Mullen, General Manager, Sean Riordan, General Manager, Chris Ratchford, Assistant Director, Australian Competition and Consumer Commission (ACCC), Cristina Cifuentes, former ACCC Commissioner and AER Board member, Australia; Philip Cullum, Senior Adviser, Imogen Hartcher-O'Brien, Director of Regulatory Strategy and Principal Lawyer, Australian Energy Regulator (AER), Australia; Yoshihiro Nemoto, Regulatory Governance Superintendent, Vanessa Da Silva Santos, Regulation Specialist, Cynthia Ruas Vieira Brayer, Chief Advisor at the Superintendency of Infrastructure Concession, Ali Murshed, Superintendent in Governance, Planning and Institutional Articulation, National Land Transportation Regulatory Agency (ANTT), Brazil; Scott Streiner, CEO and Chair, Canadian Transportation Agency (CTA), Canada; Susanna Metsälampi, Head of Department, Transport and Communications Agency (TRAFICOM), Finland; Laurent Toustou, Advisor to the Economy, Markets and Digital Director, Pierre Dubreuil, Head of Data Driven Regulation Unit - Internet, Press, Post and Users, Antoine Samba, Head of International Affairs Unit – European and International Affairs, Marta Boucher, International Affairs Advisor – European and International Affairs, Electronic Communications, Postal and Print Media Distribution Regulatory Authority (ARCEP), France; Anne Yvrande Billon, former Vice President, Transport Regulatory Authority (ART), France; Miyuki Tsuchiya, Policy Officer, the Energy Regulatory Commission (CRE), France; Matthew Crowe, former Director of Office of Evidence & Assessment, Fiona O'Rourke, Senior Scientific Officer, Jason Larkin, Data Scientist, Environmental Protection Agency (EPA), Ireland; Antonio Nicita, Commissioner for Telecommunication, Postal and Media Services, and Professor of Economics, Telecommunications Regulator (AGCOM), Italy; Andrea Camanzi, President, Assunta Luisa Perrotti, Head of Cabinet, Transport Regulation Authority (ART), Italy; Julio Salvador Jacome, General Manager, Abel Rodriguez, former Manager of Policy and Economic Analysis, Ricardo De La Cruz Sandoval, Senior Specialist of Economic Analysis and acting Manager of Policy and Economic Analysis, Energy and Mining Regulator (Osinergmin), Peru; Sergio Cifuentes, General Manager, Romina Alania Recarte, Regulatory Specialist,

Telecommunications Regulator (OSIPTEL), Peru; Ana Barreto Albuquerque, Executive Board Member, The Water and Waste Services Regulation Authority (ERSAR), Portugal.

Table of contents

FIGURES

TABLES

Follow OECD Publications on:

http://twitter.com/OECD_Pubs

http://www.facebook.com/OECDPublications

http://www.linkedin.com/groups/OECD-Publications-4645871

http://www.youtube.com/oecdilibrary

http://www.oecd.org/oecddirect/

Abbreviations and acronyms

ACCC	Australian Competition and Consumer Commission
ADLC	French Competition Authority (*Autorité de la Concurrence*)
AER	Australian Energy Regulator
AGCOM	Telecommunications Regulator (*Autorità per le Garanzie nelle Comunicazioni*)
AMF	Financial Markets Authority (*Autorité des Marchés Financiers*)
ANTT	National Land Transportation Regulatory Agency (*Agência Nacional de Transportes Terrestres*)
ARCEP	Electronic Communications, Postal and Print Media Distribution Regulatory Authority (*Autorité de régulation des communications électroniques, des postes et de la distribution de la presse*)
ARJEL	French Gaming Authority (*Autorité de Régulation des Jeux en Ligne*)
ART	French Regulatory Transport Authority (*Autorité de Régulation des Transports*)
ART	Transport Regulation Authority (*Autorità di Regolazione dei Trasporti*)
BEIS	Department for Business, Energy and Industrial Strategy
CNIL	Data Protection Authority (*Commission Nationale de l'Informatique et des Libertés*)
CRE	Energy Regulatory Commission (*Commission de Régulation de l'Energie*)
CSA	French Broadcasting Authority (*Conseil Supérieur de l'Audiovisuel*)
CTA	Canadian Transportation Agency
EPA	Environmental Protection Agency
ERSAR	The Water and Waste Services Regulation Authority (*Entidade Reguladora dos Serviços de Águas e Resíduos*)
EU	European Union

NER	Network of Economic Regulators
OECD	Organisation for Economic Cooperation and Development
Osinergmin	Energy and Mining Regulator (*Organismo Supervisor de la Inversión en Energía y Minería*)
OSIPTEL	Telecommunications Regulator (*Organismo Supervisor de Inversión Privada en Telecomunicaciones*)
RHC	United Kingdom Regulatory Horizons Council
RPC	Regulatory Policy Committee
TRAFICOM	Transport and Communications Agency (*Liikenne- ja viestintävirasto*)

Executive summary

Emerging technologies have enabled the development of new products, services and business models that were hardly conceivable just a few years ago. Their pace and scope continue to have an astonishing impact on markets and societies. Furthermore, the COVID-19 pandemic has illustrated the strategic importance of developing more agile and co-ordinated approaches to improve both responsiveness and resilience in fast-changing environments. In this context, governments face the task of promoting innovation and maximising its benefits for all, as well as mitigating risks that arise. While doing so, governments and regulators face four interrelated challenges:

1. keeping pace with change: digital technologies tend to develop faster than the regulation governing them, and thus there is a continuous need to stay up to date with technological progress and its effects;

2. designing "fit-for-purpose" regulatory frameworks to respond to the encroachment of digital platforms into various sectors, as well as changes in the traditional delineations between consumers and providers;

3. tackling regulatory enforcement challenges, as traditional enforcement might not be effective in the context of emerging technologies;

4. addressing the transversal and transboundary dimensions of these technologies, since digitalisation gives business global reach and has a consequential effect on jurisdictional boundaries.

The report looks at these challenges and how regulators seek to address them through two main lenses. First, regulators are identifying and seizing opportunities offered by emerging technologies to enhance the design and delivery of regulations. Second, regulators are demonstrating agility in adapting their own governance and regulatory frameworks in this fast-changing environment. To illustrate these phenomena, the report brings together fourteen case studies that span nine countries and a wide range of sectors (communication, transport, energy, environmental protection) and provide concrete examples of how regulators are responding to innovation in the sectors that they oversee.

From the case studies, it emerges that regulators are increasingly harnessing the benefits of innovative technologies, by seizing opportunities that ultimately reduce information asymmetries with market actors and increase regulators' capacity. Some examples include real-time monitoring of traffic flows, use of drones to support risk-based inspections, or data analysis and data interpretation software. In addition, data-driven regulation provides significant opportunities to improve transparency (including with stakeholders as varied as consumers, businesses, policy makers, and local authorities), reduce information asymmetries in regulated industries and create incentives to steer the market in the right direction. Embedding the digital tools for data-driven regulation in the compliance process also leads to savings for market operators, which in turn are passed to the consumers and the wider economy.

With regard to regulators' agility in adapting their own governance arrangements, resourcing and regulatory frameworks, the case studies highlight approaches and practices across a number of dimensions.

- *Fit-for-purpose legal and regulatory frameworks:* changes brought about by emerging technologies, such as the blurring of traditional sector lines or the rise of "prosumers" have led regulators to assess the relevance of the status quo. Such assessments have required regulators to take into account elements such as new products and services, the pace of disruption, behaviour changes and evolving stakeholder preferences. In some jurisdictions, in-built flexible design has allowed regulatory frameworks to retain their relevance; such cases may provide useful lessons for the development of adaptive, responsive regulatory approaches.

- *Mandates and powers aligned with sector needs:* the volume of data gathered through the use of new technologies grows continuously and at an unprecedented pace, raising a number of challenges for regulators and policy makers. The regulation of digital markets, given their complexity, requires appropriate inspection and data collection powers, data analytics capabilities, and enforcement powers, among others. Having the right "toolbox" and consumer-centric approach may require a reform or an update or the regulator's mandate and legal powers.

- *Adequate internal structure, resourcing and skills:* emerging technologies and related market evolutions can prompt changes in the internal governance, resourcing and structure of regulators. In some cases, operational change is driven by measures such as the introduction of an innovation-specific department. In other cases, the shift in regulatory approach or market practices is reflected in a holistic organisational overhaul. Across the board, there is need to update skills in the workforce and to implement change management strategies for organisational culture to adapt to and support these changes.

- *Ensuring foresight:* regulators across jurisdictions have set up teams or committees with a focus on innovation and emerging technologies. Such teams can help articulate a forward-looking perspective and channel it into the regulator's strategy and everyday activities. They can also support regulators in providing inputs to government policy. In order to remain in sync with the sectors, regulators need to embrace an internal culture whereby innovation and new ways of approaching problems are considered business as usual. The role of leadership is crucial in mainstreaming such a vision and culture across the agency.

Embracing enhanced co-operation: Digitalisation enables businesses to have a global reach, just as new business models disregard traditional boundaries between sectors. There are a number of examples of co-operation among regulators at national and international level as well as across sectors. On an international level, regulatory co-operation comes in many forms and types, ranging from prescriptive and formal arrangements such as regulatory harmonisation imposed by international treaties, to information exchanges among regulators through informal working-level arrangements or the participation in trans-governmental networks of regulators.

The case studies show that, given their unique position at the forefront of interaction with and oversight of regulated markets, regulators must stay abreast of market transformations and act accordingly. Moreover, the COVID-19 pandemic has created an urgent need for regulators and policy makers to adapt their approaches and further stimulate innovation.

1 The impact of emerging technologies on economic regulators

This chapter highlight trends and findings on the impact of emerging technologies on economic regulators, based on detailed case studies prepared by members of the OECD Network of Economic Regulators. It describes how emerging technologies represent a sea change for regulators, how regulators are using emerging technologies and new tools such as data-driven regulation for better regulatory delivery. The chapter also highlights key dimensions to consider when assessing whether regulators' governance frameworks are fit for the purpose in the context of the Fourth Industrial Revolution, including legal and regulatory frameworks, mandates and powers, resources and internal organisation, foresight capacity and national, regional or international co-ordination.

Emerging technologies: a sea change for regulators

Emerging technologies have enabled the development of new products, services and business models that were hardly conceivable just a few years ago. Their pace and scope continue to have an astonishing impact on markets and societies (OECD, 2019[1]) (OECD, 2020[2]). At the same time, emerging technologies can bring with them adverse effects, for instance by significantly disrupting labour in traditional markets or by marginalising fragile populations. They also raise profound challenges in terms of data governance - for instance regarding data privacy, discrimination, or the ethical use of data.

Regulation is essential to mitigate the risks of emerging technologies, while promoting innovation and maximising benefits for all. In this context, it is clear that sweeping technological advancements create a sea change for regulators.

Governments and regulatory authorities face a series of interrelated challenges with regard to emerging technologies (OECD, 2019[3]):

- First: *keeping pace with change*. Regulators are struggling to keep pace with disruptions brought by emerging technologies. Regulatory frameworks might not be agile enough to accommodate the expeditious technological development and, in many cases, current rules might be outdated and no longer relevant. Regulators may also lack knowledge of how emerging technologies affect market places and society more broadly;

- Second: *designing "fit-for-purpose" regulatory frameworks*. Traditional regulatory frameworks, often based on market-specific rationales, may not be a good fit in the context of emerging technologies. They challenge regulators' mandates and remits by blurring the traditional definition of markets as well as, in some instances, between consumers and producers. Tackling this new reality requires co-ordination, harmonisation, or integration of regulatory practices, often demanding a multidisciplinary perspective. For instance, digital platforms that are increasingly performing similar functions to media businesses challenge the traditional approaches to media regulation. In addition, the development of data-driven markets creates the risk of market failures (such as implicit transactions, incomplete markets, information asymmetries, hold-up and locked-in phenomena) that should be carefully addressed by governments;

- Third: *regulatory enforcement challenges*. Emerging technologies such as artificial intelligence challenge regulatory enforcement by questioning the traditional notion of liability, due to difficulties in apportioning and attributing responsibility for damage caused to end users by the use of such technology. Another example of the enforcement challenge is provided by the difficulty to enforce copyright/property rights in digital markets: data-driven businesses have given rise to a fundamentally new way to distribute content, challenging traditional copyright frameworks. Copyright infringements are made possible by the intrinsic nature of digital information goods, which are easy to replicate;

- Fourth: *institutional and transboundary challenges*. The market-specific rationale behind traditional institutional and regulatory frameworks shows its limits when dealing with the transversal dimension of emerging technologies, especially in digital markets. Most data-driven markets pay no regard to national boundaries, enabling companies to "forum shop" regarding their physical presence or their tax or data protection policies. The fragmentation of regulatory frameworks across jurisdictions can also generate barriers to the spread of beneficial digital innovations as it can be difficult for business to navigate jurisdictional complexities. Moreover, because of the transboundary nature of markets and business models, competition issues become increasingly international in scope and raise strong challenges as regards antitrust enforcement. These characteristics call for strong international regulatory co-operation, notably to prevent companies from taking undue advantage of the fragmentation of regulatory frameworks.

The challenges outlined above create a context where governments face growing public and political pressure to engage differently with innovation. Responding to these expectations requires a careful balancing act between enabling the development of useful technologies, and ensuring that any downside risks are effectively managed, both with regard to the development of new regulations and their enforcement. This is also true for economic regulators that are tasked with providing stability and predictability to markets and investors, protecting consumers and ensuring quality and access to services, as they are called to guarantee positive outcomes for the market and respond to citizen expectations. In addition, regulatory authorities can play a critical role in supporting policy makers navigate the challenges and opportunities brought by emerging technologies and choose the right regulatory (or non-regulatory) approach. On account of having their "finger on the pulse" of markets, economic regulators are ideally positioned to observe technology trends, understand their potential transformative impacts and underlying challenges.

To shed light on these issues, this report draws together case studies of practices by members of the OECD's Network of Economic Regulators (NER) across network sectors (e-communications, energy, transport and water) from nine countries (Australia, Brazil, Canada, Finland, France, Ireland, Italy, Peru, Portugal). The 14 case studies provide insights as to how emerging technologies are shaping the future of regulators, and how regulators are responding to these changes.

The case studies show, on the one hand, how regulators are using emerging technologies to deliver regulations more effectively and efficiently. The examples highlight regulators' efforts in harnessing the opportunities provided by digital transformation to strengthen their regulatory capacity. Technological progress can offer new innovative approaches to resource-constrained regulators and can support more agile and efficient regulation in response to innovation. Data-driven regulation provides in particular great opportunities to improve transparency, reduce information asymmetries in regulated industries and foster the incentives to steer the market in the right direction. On the other hand, the case studies illustrate some of the challenges that emerging technologies pose to the governance and performance of regulators; as well as how regulators are addressing these new dimensions by turning them into opportunities to update regulatory frameworks, review ways of working internally and with others, and to align their capacities with new expectations.

Using emerging technologies for better regulatory delivery

Emerging technologies grant new opportunities to resource-constrained regulators to strengthen their regulatory capacity. Regulators can capitalise on a wide of range of technologies to develop more agile, dynamic and efficient regulations that keep pace with the transformative changes generated by emerging technologies. Enforcement activities can also greatly benefit from the advantages offered by new technological tools.

Harnessing the power of data and digital tools to improve regulation

The digital transformation benefits also the regulators themselves: by employing new technologies, regulators can reduce information asymmetries with market players. These technologies can be leveraged to extend capacity to collect, access, share and use existing data on regulated markets (both upstream and downstream) and open the "black box" of monopolies. The augmented availability of data on issues that were previously imperfectly observable, or only observable at significant administrative cost, provides opportunities to improve monitoring and supervision (e.g. real time and continuous monitoring of compliance) and more effective enforcement of policies.

Governments and regulatory authorities are increasingly relying on data-driven approaches to improve regulation,[1] as part of broader efforts to implement digital government approaches (OECD, 2019[4]). The so-called "data-driven regulation" developed by the French telecom regulator (ARCEP) and the French transport regulator (ART) offers a good illustration of this trend. Both regulators regard "data-driven regulation" as a powerful tool to complement existing regulatory mechanisms and to develop more dynamic, agile and technology-neutral regulations along three main avenues.

Firstly, "data-driven" regulation allows the collection and analysis of (big) data, which in turn enables regulators to monitor markets more closely and, as such, can lead to better and faster decisions based on a comprehensive knowledge of the regulated environment. ART France is for example running regular data collection campaigns to monitor the quality of regulated services and to inform benchmarking exercises in the transport sector.

Secondly, digital tools underpinning data-driven regulation can significantly improve supervision, inspections and enforcement activities through the collection and analysis of increasingly granular datasets. In conjunction with improving the monitoring of imperfectly observable outcomes, the tools enable better real-time data collection for compliance monitoring. Similarly to ART France, ARCEP is developing a digital tool to monitor national fixed network coverage at a level of granularity that was not previously possible (the objective is to provide detailed information at the individual address level).

Lastly, regulators can use data-driven regulation to provide personalised and tailor-made information (e.g. on service quality) to increase transparency, and to allow stakeholders (consumers, businesses, policymakers, local authorities, etc.) to make more informed choices. This, in turn, is expected to create incentives that steer the market in the right direction.

Two main actions have been undertaken by ARCEP in that perspective:

- The publication of maps designed through digital simulations ("*Monreseaumobile.fr*" and "*Cartefibre.arcep.fr*") which provide detailed data and information on the French operators' coverage and service quality across the country;
- A reporting platform ("*J'alerte l'Arcep*") to allow any stakeholder (individual, businesses or local authority) to report a malfunction which they experienced with a service provider - either telephone operator (fixed or mobile), internet service or postal operator.

The initiative launched by Brazil's National Land Transportation Agency (ANTT) also demonstrates that digital technologies can provide greater efficiencies in carrying out regulatory functions (such as monitoring and inspections activities). A technology-enabled project implemented by ANTT is the "Green Channel Brazil" (*Canal Verde Brasil*), an intelligent national network for the monitoring and mapping of transport flows in logistics corridors. The objective is to produce data and analysis to inform market regulation, and to improve the enforcement of freight transportation regulations.

The Peruvian Energy and Mining Regulator (OSINERGMIN) has also developed a series of initiatives directed at improving its supervision activities, such as: the collection and analysis of big data to review the information declared in the Energy Information Remission Portal (PRIE), the introduction of mobile applications for real-time monitoring, as well as the use of drones to support risk-based inspections. These initiatives have significantly improved supervision capacities and contributed to a reduction in average supervision costs, freeing up resources to enhance other activities.

Likewise, the Irish Environmental Protection Agency (EPA) has developed a series of initiatives to improve its monitoring of urban wastewater treatment plants in Ireland. The EPA invested in different digital tools to build a data management system delivering timely and precise information on water treatment plants' efficiency.

It emerges from the case studies that, by becoming "active users" of new technologies, regulators can ensure that the compliance process is streamlined, and thus the associated regulatory burden for operators can be reduced. Not only can this lead to better compliance, and greater consumer protection, but the financial benefits of operators which stem from regulatory-related cost savings are passed on to consumers and the wider economy.

How to look ahead?

The case studies illustrate that the use of digital technologies with the aim of improving regulation also raises some challenges that should be carefully addressed, including (but not limited to):

- The scope, volume and quality of data provided by the market to regulators need to increase to allow for a comprehensive approach and analysis. This should be supported by an enhanced access to, sharing and use of data. This entails a review and reinforcement of data governance arrangements at the strategic, tactical and delivery levels (see (OECD, 2019[4])), including the:

  1. adaptation of regulatory frameworks in order to make sure that market players produce the relevant data in an appropriate fashion (whilst at the same time ensuring that no disproportionate administrative burden is placed on market operators, especially on smaller market players); and the

  2. development of new analytical skills, together with the deployment of necessary digital infrastructure to support data generation, collection, storage, management, sharing and dissemination;

- Regulatory structures, allocation of resources, methods and practices are likely to change with the development of data-driven regulation. Nonetheless, the repositioning of stakeholders such as end-users in the regulation equation holds the potential to challenge the traditional paradigms governing the institutional organisation of regulation;

- Co-operation between regulators is key to share expertise, build capacity and identify good practices. In that perspective, eight French regulators (Competition Authority (ADLC), Financial Market Authority (AMF), Telecommunications Regulatory Body (ARCEP), Data Protection Authority (CNIL), Energy Regulatory Body (CRE), Broadcasting Authority (CSA), Gaming Authority (ARJEL) and Transport Regulatory Authority (ART) issued a dedicated memorandum which outlines existing practices, and discusses some of the challenges raised by data-driven regulation. Similarly, ANTT is also relying on co-operation with other government agencies to develop its intelligent national transport network. Yet, such co-ordination could be particularly challenging notably in terms of interoperability and data-sharing policies[2].

Ensuring fit for purpose governance for the regulation of emerging technologies

New technologies offer significant opportunities for regulators to enhance the efficiency of their activities. However, the disruptive changes induced by emerging technologies also present challenges to regulators. These are reflected in the pacing problem and whether governments and regulators can keep abreast of changes in markets and of the needs of the economy and society, but also in other dimensions of a regulator's governance. For example, not only may the legal and regulatory framework be misaligned with new market characteristics and business practices, but regulators' own mandates and functions may not be adequate to discharge their duties in the new context. The evolution of markets and sectors may also inspire regulators to rethink their own internal organisation, or pose challenges with regard to their own capacity or resourcing, as specialised skills are required to carry out new functions. Further, emerging technologies demand more collaborative regulation, both at international and national level.

Are legal and regulatory frameworks fit for purpose?

Across sectors of the economy, new technologies have changed industries and created new markets, altered the way in which consumers interact with operators, and increased the expectations that consumers have from the market actors and the regulators. In the electricity sector, for example, the rise of prosumers (actors who are both consumers and producers of electrical power) have revolutionised how market actors are defined and how grids are required to function. In the transport sector, for instance, a new market was created by app-based ride-sharing, which required regulators from different sectors to closely collaborate (transport, financial, health and safety) and changed the status and nature of the various users (for instance, the driver is the customer of the ride-sharing app, but also the provider of a service for the ultimate user of the taxi service). As outlined by the AGCOM case study, digitalisation has given rise to a new convergence in telecommunications, media markets and digital platforms, in which many components of the digital ecosystem are closely interrelated. This convergence questions whether the existing regulatory mandates and remits are still fit for purpose.

An example of how to tackle the critical challenge of assessing the relevance of a regulatory framework developed over the years for today's economy is provided by the "Regulatory Modernisation Initiative" (RMI) undertaken by Canadian Transportation Agency (CTA). The RMI was an ambitious and over-arching project intended to review and update every regulation the CTA administers, with the goal of ensuring that the regulations keep pace with changes in business models, user expectations, disruptive technologies and best practices in the regulatory field. As such, the initiative looked at the substance, form and delivery of regulation. For this purpose, the CTA designed a multi-step process, building in four consultation phases: one each on accessible transportation, air transportation, air passenger protection, and rail transportation. Between 2016 and 2020, a number of reforms were designed and implemented, consolidating and updating existing regulations in order to alleviate burden on industry and provide benefits to consumers.

Similarly, in response to significant transformations in the telecommunications sector, the Australian Competition and Consumer Commission (ACCC) launched a study in 2018 to assess whether the current regulatory arrangements remained adequate, looking forward over a five year period. The study found that the ACCC has a comprehensive and flexible set of tools at its disposal and that the regulatory framework remains broadly "fit-for-purpose".

In addition to questioning the relevance of regulatory frameworks and approaches, new technologies also disrupt traditional definitions of markets. For example, as identified by ART France, this is apparent in the transport sector: as digitalisation is more widespread, there is less delimitation between the services offered within the sector. Consequently, regulators are required to analyse whether the current service delineations within the same sector are still adequate, or whether a more holistic approach is to be considered. These definitions may also have important implications in terms of competition policy: redefining the market boundaries can lead to changes in the definition of relevant markets and thus can reshape the structure of an industry, either nationally or regionally.

Overall, the case studies highlight that regulators need to take into account a number of factors: new products and services in the markets they regulate, the pace of the disruptive developments, the societal and consumer behaviour changes as a reaction to the emerging technologies, as well as evolving stakeholder preferences. In this fast-changing environment, regulators must remain alert to market developments. In some jurisdictions, in-built flexible design has allowed for regulatory frameworks to retain their relevance; such cases may provide useful lessons for the development of adaptive, responsive regulatory approaches. Furthermore, whilst it is clear that the regulators are at the forefront of experiencing the changes brought by emerging technologies, they will need to collaborate with national governments and parliaments to ensure that the legal framework which defines the remit and powers of the regulators remains relevant to the realities of the market in which they operate. Comprehensive reviews of legal frameworks and institutional arrangements may also be initiated by governments.

Are regulator mandates and powers aligned with data-driven businesses?

The volume of personal and non-personal data gathered through the use of new technologies grows continuously at an unprecedented pace, raising a number of challenges for regulators and policy makers

(OECD, 2019[5]). Data comes in many forms, and its value is derived from its owners' and users' ability to classify and analyse it – this, in turn, provides unique insights into the consumers' movements, interests, or preferences (OECD, 2013[6]).

One of the many manifestations of the advent of big data is the ability of market players to use data to personalise and target products and services to consumers ("data profiling"). These practices may lead to online information distortions, whether through online advertising or through the use of search engines and social networks. The Italian e-communications regulator, AGCOM, identified big data and disinformation strategies as a priority issue to be solved. Following a market review, AGCOM launched "technical committee ("*tavolo tecnico*") on pluralism and fair information on digital platforms", in close co-operation with large market players such as Google, Facebook and national audio-visual providers. An outcome of AGCOM's initiative was the first issue of "*Guidelines for equal access to online platforms during the election campaign for the political elections*". AGCOM did not go into the remit of deciding on the authenticity of information on digital platforms - but rather, the technical committee focused its work on issuing guidelines for media operators, on matters such as methodologies for classifying and detecting online disinformation, tools and techniques used for fact-checking, or monitoring systems for economic advertising aimed at financing mis-informative content. The work also served to highlight that the regulator's mandate and scope of action had to adapt to these guidelines, and to take more steps on public education in relation to the distribution of "fake news" and misinformation through the online channels. Actions such as this exemplify changes in the mandate of regulators, and show how a more inclusive way of devising regulation, through the direct implication of market players, can promote compliance, and raise awareness about the impact of digital and data economy.

The regulation of digital markets, given their complexity, requires an appropriate toolbox, including but not limited to: inspection and data collection powers (so that regulators can request and receive sufficient information in real time and in relevant shape), data analytics capabilities (so that they can interpret the data), and enforcement powers (so that they can take action when breaches have been identified). Moreover, as identified by AGCOM in the "Internet services and on-line advertising" inquiry (AGCOM, n.d.[7]), a horizontal regulatory perspective which puts the consumer at the centre is needed. Having the appropriate "toolbox" and consumer-centric approach may require a reform or an update or the regulator's mandate and legal powers.

Moreover, data-driven markets present specific and important challenges which may question the rationale for regulatory intervention. On the one hand, network externalities, the capacity to scale without mass and the economies of scope characterising online platforms can give rise to natural monopoly conditions and create barriers to entry for potential competitors monopolies (Jens Prüfer, 2017[8]). This in turn, can bring substantial risks that excessive prices and lack of innovation will follow. Such phenomena might call for new regulation of digital markets, as advocated by the ACCC's Digital Platforms Enquiry (ACCC, 2019[9]). Nonetheless, the same economic properties might shift in favour of innovative entrants and stimulate competition. Digital goods offer avenues for new entrants to grow rapidly and gain market shares over incumbents once they bring a new product to market, often with few employees, few tangible assets and limited geographic footprint. These counteracting effects might confuse the rationale for regulatory action as any initiative will influence the nature of competition between the incumbent and (potential) new entrants.

Are regulators adequately organised and resourced?

Beyond the regulatory framework and legal attributes of the regulator, emerging technologies and linked market evolutions can prompt changes in the internal governance, resourcing and structure of regulators. In some cases, operational change is driven by measures such as the introduction of an innovation-specific department. In other cases, the shift in regulatory approach or shift in market practices are reflected in a holistic organisational overhaul. Across the board, there is pressure to update skills in the workforce of the authority.

For instance, in Finland, a number of institutional reforms were carried out to support the adoption of the concept of "mobility as a service" (MAAS), which puts the consumer at the centre of the transport system, as a key pillar of the country's transport policy. To accompany this new paradigm efficiently, Finland not only merged all transport regulators so that one single entity has an overview of the transport sector as a whole, but also reorganised the regulator so that the agency follows a process-based matrix organigram. The new organisational structure at Traficom allows for sharing of know-how and best practices from different fields, ultimately benefiting the sector as a whole. In practice, immediate effects of the internal reform were the streamlining of regulation practices and processes for transport registers, licenses, consumer rights, and data disclosure obligations. Such restructurings may need to be accompanied by changes in legislation.

In addition, as market actors are requested to share increasing amounts of data with regulators, there is a need for regulators to streamline and optimise their supervision, inspections and enforcement activities. On data collection specifically, this will include elimination of duplicated data requests, creation of central databases, or formalisation of responsibilities among departments that interact with the same regulated entity. For instance, one of the aims of the internal reform process designed and implemented by Portugal's Water and Waste Services Regulation Entity ERSAR, aimed among its objectives to consolidate interactions with each regulated entity in one department – rather than spread out across the agency. This change led to a higher satisfaction of regulated entities with regard to the follow up capacity of the regulator, but the example also highlights the need for an explicit change management strategy in the case of such internal reform, to anticipate and manage status quo bias and resistance to change. Agility as well as openness to the use of new technologies in the process of regulation may require explicit focus by agency leadership on creating a forward looking and flexible working culture.

Finally, emerging technologies have undoubtedly introduced new functions and types of activities to be carried out by regulators. This may place pressure both on the overall resources of the regulator and its capacity to bring necessary skills to the workforce. Moreover, regulators may already operate within administrative constraints with regard to headcount or competitiveness of salaries due to general public administration rules and frameworks. The example of the Australian Energy Regulator (AER) is an encouraging one with regard to adequate resourcing of a regulatory authority in line with increasing functions and the complexity of markets. Following the findings of a government-commissioned study, the staffing of the regulator rose by about 75% between 2017 and 2019. This increase was managed through the AER's Strategic Transformation Programme that translated the report's recommendations into a detailed action plan.

How to look ahead?

Keeping up with market developments and having the capacity to analyse latest evolutions are not easy tasks given the pace of change and technical specialisation of government bodies. This gap becomes even more pronounced when attempting to stay ahead of - instead of catching up with – the wave. To bridge these gaps, regulators across jurisdictions have started to set up units or committees with a focus on innovation and emerging technologies. Such dedicated teams can enhance capacity to oversee ever-changing markets and to deliver effectively against regulators' objectives in these contexts; they can also help articulate a forward-looking perspective, and can be tasked with channelling this into the regulator's strategy, priorities, objectives and every day activities. These teams can also support regulators formulate inputs to government policy, for example when important trends or forthcoming issues can be anticipated.

Nonetheless, in order to remain in sync with the sectors, regulators need to embrace an internal culture whereby innovation and new ways of approaching problems are considered business as usual - rather than employing a siloed function separate from the organisation in which they sit. The role of leadership in mainstreaming such a vision and culture across the agency is key. Similarly, the experience of regulators rapidly adjusting their ways of working and formulating new goals in the context of the COVID-19 pandemic are proof that such agility and outcome-focus are within reach of regulatory institutions (OECD, 2020[10]).

The Foresight Committee (*Comité de prospective)* created by the French Commission for Regulation of Energy (CRE) is an example of regulator-led body which aims to identify long-term issues and forward-looking solutions, in this case in the energy sector. The two-fold objectives of the Committee are to: i) provide expertise to CRE and energy stakeholders; ii) implement a successful energy transition and to put the digital revolution at the service of all electricity and gas consumers, in a multidisciplinary and collective prospective action. It is tasked with fulfilling these functions with both a medium- and long-term vision (2030 and 2050).

The CRE Foresight Committee is also an example of wide stakeholder engagement, as it brings together a multidisciplinary team, including the industry, the academia, consumer groups, consulting firms and representatives from local and national authorities. In this way, it not only ensures a well-rounded perspective of the sector, but also builds consensus on solutions and proposals from an early stage.

Other declinations of such initiatives include, at internal level within regulatory agencies, the creation of the "Innovation and pilot projects" team at Portugal's ERSE, that will be tasked with monitoring market evolutions, carrying our pilot activities and upscaling them. Another example is brought by the United Kingdom Regulatory Horizons Council (RHC) that is established as an independent expert committee that identifies the implications of technological innovation, and provides government with impartial, expert advice on the regulatory reform required to support its rapid and safe introduction. The RHC was created by the Department for Business, Energy and Industrial Strategy (BEIS) rather than a sector regulator, and accordingly its scope is not sectorial (Regulatory Horizons Council, 2020[11]).

The creation of such departments/hubs enables regulators to create specialist teams focused on the inclusion of data-driven means into the fabric of the organisation, both at regulatory and organisational levels. In addition, the level of senior management involvement in data-driven industry developments (for instance designating a director general for data or innovation) gives confidence to the markets and to consumers that the regulator is anchored in the day-today realities of the sector.

Are co-operation and co-ordination revamped in the new context?

Digitalisation enables businesses to have a global reach, just as new business models disregard traditional boundaries between sectors. The case studies include a number of examples of co-operation at national and international level. For instance, ARCEP and ART France, alongside six other national regulators have developed a common national strategy for data-driven regulation in a public memorandum (ARCEP, 2019[12]). The document lays out the regulators' common views and good practices on the use of data, and updates stakeholders on the progress made on data-driven regulation. This approach has several impacts: it provides transparency to market players on regulatory paradigms, and it enhances consumer awareness and participation, which in turn has a positive impact on the consumers' ability to make more informed choices.

A similar approach on national cross-sectoral co-operation was employed by ANTT in Brazil through technical co-operation agreements. ANTT's experience shows that an integrated approach among transport regulators (land, rail and ports) and employment data sharing platforms brings efficiencies not only in relation to the pace of regulation, but has direct impact on the cost of transport of goods.

On an international level, regulatory co-operation comes in many forms and types (OECD, 2013[13]). These range from prescriptive and formal arrangements such as regulatory harmonisation governed by international treaties, to information exchanges among regulators through informal working-level arrangements or the participation in trans-governmental networks of regulators. In addition, platforms such as the OECD's Network of Economic Regulators (NER) or the Regulatory Policy Committee (RPC) offer the opportunity for continuous dialogue and for comparing and debating developments in regulatory practices, ultimately aimed at developing "a common regulatory language".

Furthermore, the fragmentation of regulatory practices across jurisdictions could mean, in simple terms, a reduction of regulatory capacity. For example, there is a risk that uneven regulatory playing fields create misalignment of incentives which can create market failures, leading to inadequate consumer protection, or create unnecessary burdens on industry. In addition to operational and effective market supervision concerns, jurisdictional discrepancies also mean that it may be difficult for regulators to bring legal proceedings or issue enforcement action. The EU stands out as having developed regulatory harmonisation and as working towards ensuring a level playing field across the jurisdictions of its members stated, so that the "four fundamental freedoms"[3] of the single market are protected (OECD, 2019[14]).

Despite these challenges, the case studies bring us examples of effective co-operation among different jurisdictions – either in a project-by-project basis, or on a sector-wide initiative. For instance, in creating the regulations behind the Regulatory Modernization Initiative, CTA collaborated with counterparts from the USA and the EU. Also, ARCEP collaborates with the network of French-speaking telecommunications regulators (Fratel) and published a joint document on mobile service and coverage. The breadth and depth of collaborative initiatives among regulators suggest that there is appetite at national and international level for the development of creative solutions that would lead to regulatory alignment, and for broad engagement with players across the ecosystem. OECD forums such as the Network of Economic Regulators can continue to be a catalyst for such engagement.

Way forward

The case studies highlight that regulatory authorities are in a unique position, at the forefront of interaction with consumers, business, and government, and with direct oversight of markets that deliver essential services to citizens and the economy. They are characterised by technical expertise and organisational agility, making them essential players of the regulatory and policy ecosystems. The case studies provide an in-depth look at the efforts employed by regulators to harness and encompass emerging technologies into their activities at national and international level. A key conclusion that surfaces is that as emerging technologies evolve, regulators rethink their approaches and adapt their internal governance, towards becoming more agile, iterative and collaborative, so that they are equipped to face the challenges brought about by the Fourth Industrial Revolution.

Looking ahead, the case studies bring to the fore the strategic importance of on the one hand developing more agile and co-ordinated approaches to increase responsiveness and resilience in fast changing environments and, on the other, capitalising further on the opportunities provided by emerging technologies. As the COVID-19 pandemic has exacerbated this challenge, regulators now face a pressing and urgent need to adapt their approaches and to further stimulate innovation.

References

ACCC (2019), *Digital Platforms Inquiry - Final Report*, [9]
    https://www.accc.gov.au/publications/digital-platforms-inquiry-final-report.

AGCOM (n.d.), *Indagine conoscitiva sul settore dei servizi internet e sulla pubblicità online*, [7]
    https://www.agcom.it/documents/10179/540203/Allegato+21-01-2014+2/9376a211-ebb2-
    4df6-83ea-282f731faaf2?version=1.1.

ARCEP (2019), *ARCEP Press release - Data-driven regulation, Cooperation between* [12]
    Regulators, Eight regulators publish the fruit of their common approach to data-driven
    regulation, https://en.arcep.fr/news/press-releases/p/n/cooperation-between-regulators.html.

Jens Prüfer, C. (2017), *Competing with Big Data*, [8]
    https://research.tilburguniversity.edu/en/publications/competing-with-big-data.

OECD (2020), *OECD Global Conference on Governance Innovation: Summary Records*, [15]
    http://www.oecd.org/gov/regulatory-policy/global-conference-on-governance-innovation-
    summary-record-2020.pdf.

OECD (2020), *OECD work on emerging technologies and regulation*, OECD, [2]
    http://www.oecd.org/gov/regulatory-policy/regulation-and-emerging-technologies.htm.

OECD (2020), *When the going gets tough, the tough get going: How economic regulators bolster* [10]
    the resilience of network industries in response to the COVID-19 crisis, OECD, Paris,
    http://www.oecd.org/coronavirus/policy-responses/when-the-going-gets-tough-the-tough-get-
    going-how-economic-regulators-bolster-the-resilience-of-network-industries-in-response-to-
    the-covid-19-crisis-cd8915b1/#biblio-d1e1202.

OECD (2019), *"Data in the digital age"*, OECD Going Digital Policy Note, OECD, Paris, [5]
    https://www.oecd.org/going-digital/data-in-the-digital-age.pdf.

OECD (2019), *Better Regulation Practices across the European Union*, OECD Publishing, Paris, [14]
    https://dx.doi.org/10.1787/9789264311732-en.

OECD (2019), *Going Digital: Shaping Policies, Improving Lives*, OECD Publishing, Paris, [1]
    https://dx.doi.org/10.1787/9789264312012-en.

OECD (2019), *Regulatory effectiveness in the era of digitalisation*, [3]
    https://www.oecd.org/gov/regulatory-policy/Regulatory-effectiveness-in-the-era-of-
    digitalisation.pdf.

OECD (2019), *The Path to Becoming a Data-Driven Public Sector*, OECD Digital Government [4]
    Studies, OECD Publishing, Paris, https://dx.doi.org/10.1787/059814a7-en.

OECD (2013), *International Regulatory Co-operation: Addressing Global Challenges*, OECD [13]
    Publishing, Paris, https://dx.doi.org/10.1787/9789264200463-en.

OECD (2013), *The OECD Privacy Network*, OECD, Paris, [6]
    https://www.oecd.org/sti/ieconomy/oecd_privacy_framework.pdf.

Regulatory Horizons Council (2020), *Charter*, [11]
https://assets.publishing.service.gov.uk/government/uploads/system/uploads/attachment_dat
a/file/881237/RHC_Charter.pdf.

Notes

[1] This trend was highlighted, in particular, during the OECD Global Conference on Governance Innovation (http://www.oecd.org/fr/gov/politique-reglementaire/oecd-global-conference-on-governance-innovation.htm) held in January 2020 (OECD, 2020[15]).

[2] OECD has his conducted work on the role of data in creating conditions that improve public services, increase the effectiveness of public spending and inform ethical and privacy considerations. The Report on *The Path to Becoming a Data-Driven Public Sector* presents a data-driven public sector framework that can help countries or organisations assess the elements needed for using data to make better-informed decisions across public sectors (OECD, 2019[4]).

[3] The "four freedoms" of the single market are: i) free movement of goods; ii) free movement of capital; iii) freedom to establish and provide services; and iv) free movement of persons.

2 Case studies on regulator mandates and management capacity, and on the use of emerging technologies by regulators

This chapter presents a series case studies detailing regulators' responses to market transformations led by emerging technologies. The case studies span nine countries (Australia, Brazil, Canada, Finland, France, Ireland, Italy, Peru and Portugal) and a wide range of sectors (communication, transport, energy, environmental protection). They provide concrete examples of how regulators are responding to innovation in the sectors that they oversee with regard to harnessing the benefits of technological advancements for the purpose of strengthening the regulatory process, as well as how regulators are strengthening their own governance in response to the transformation of sectors under their purview.

Is Australia's economic regulatory framework for communications fit for purpose in the face of market transformation? Case study on the Australian Competition and Consumer Commission (ACCC)

Context

The overarching framework for the regulation of communications in Australia largely dates back to 1997, when a number of legislative changes took effect with the objective of opening telecommunications markets progressively to full competition and privatising Telstra (the then government-owned monopoly provider of fixed line and the largest mobile communications service provider). Most economic regulation of the sector became the responsibility of the Australian Competition and Consumer Commission (ACCC) at that time with technical regulation the responsibility of other agencies (not discussed further in this case study).[1]

The key features of the regulatory framework for communications administered by the ACCC are:

- A third-party telecommunications specific access regime under Part XIC of the Competition and Consumer Act 2010 (CCA) designed to ensure that service providers have access to monopoly and other bottleneck infrastructure to supply competitive communications services to customers, where there are limited incentives for, or significant barriers to the development of, infrastructure-based competition. Declaration of services under this instrument is subject to a "long term interests of end-users" test, which can be an outcome of an ACCC inquiry. Once a service is declared, the ACCC can determine regulated terms and conditions of upstream access in an access determination or binding rule of conduct that applies if parties are unable to agree commercially.

- A telecommunications specific anti-competitive conduct regime under Part XIB of the CCA. In addition to containing a prohibition on anti-competitive conduct, Part XIB provides the ACCC with record keeping, information disclosure and monitoring powers in relation to the telecommunications sector. The Part XIB provisions operate in addition to the general, economy-wide, anti-competitive conduct regime set out in Part IV of the CCA.

- Some other communications sector functions governed by the Telecommunications Act 1997, including provisions governing access to particular telecommunications facilities, number portability and designated interconnection services as well as provisions that safeguard competition as services transition from legacy access networks to the National Broadband Network (NBN).

Issues

In April 2018, the ACCC released its final report from a market study into the communications sector.[2] The study recognised that the sector is going through a period of significant change driven by both local developments and global technological and business trends that are changing how communications networks are designed and used to supply services.

The study looked forward over a five-year period to both examine immediate issues of concern and to form a view about the directions that policy and regulation should take. The study noted that "[t]his is to reflect the impact that new and emerging technologies and product innovations (such as Internet of Things and 5G) will have on significant segments of the communications sector. Where there are emerging impediments to competition, there may be a need for a regulatory response. Conversely, where market developments are leading to greater competition there may be an opportunity to reduce or remove existing regulation."[3]

Approach and intervention

The key finding relating to the regulatory framework from the ACCC's market study was:

> We have noted a number of issues within the communications sector…that may require regulatory responses. However…we have not found any major deficiencies in the current communications regulatory arrangements that we administer which require redress. On the contrary, our view is that the current arrangements have remained largely fit for purpose as communications markets have continued to evolve, and appear to be well suited to deal with the immediate and longer-term issues we have identified.
>
> Importantly, we have a range of regulatory tools available, if required, to deal with the issues identified with respect to NBN pricing and service standards, access to aggregation and other critical wholesale inputs, information gathering, market reporting and monitoring and consumer protection.[4]

In short, the ACCC found that the regulatory regime for communications remains fit for purpose in the face of significant market transformation and disruptive technologies. The same observation can also be made about the legal framework underpinning the ACCC's regulatory and competition roles in the sector. While there have been changes in the legal framework, most notably in 2010 to strengthen the ACCC's powers in setting upfront terms of access,[5] the broad legal framework has shown to be fit for purpose.

The ACCC noted that, to a large extent, the regulatory regime for communications has to date been one of up-front economic regulation. The ACCC has set up-front terms and conditions of access to monopoly services to promote competition in related markets, and to set a price for the monopoly service that encourages efficiency and investment. However, the ACCC did signal a change in approach to regulation as applied to newer communications services:

> "We consider that there is far less need for us to step in and set terms and conditions up-front for newer communications services".[6]

For example, the ACCC concluded that the relatively nascent Internet of Things (IoT) sector ought to be allowed to evolve without *ex ante* regulation.

While the ACCC identified a number of risks to the development of a competitive IoT sector it noted a range of government, industry and regulatory processes underway to address many of the risks.

In the context of a relative immature and fast growing sector, the ACCC considered that active involvement with relevant external processes and continued monitoring for conduct or developments of concern would be the appropriate approach to promoting investment and competition in these markets.

One issue the ACCC's study considered was how a regulatory imbalance should be addressed. That is, where regulation applies to an existing service but not a new competing service, should that imbalance be addressed and, if so, should it be addressed by applying regulation to the new service or removing regulation from the legacy one? For example, in respect of fixed line and fixed wireless broadband the ACCC concluded:

Should fixed wireless become a recognised substitute for high-speed fixed line broadband services, the need to apply consistent vertical separation regulation is likely to depend on the relative market power of firms within the sector (possibly within particular geographic areas rather than nationally), in addition to the technological substitution possibilities. However, given that fixed wireless substitution would represent an increase in competition; this would more likely signal a need to remove separation requirements on fixed line services.[7]

The ACCC recognised the rapid pace of change and the need to stay informed of developments in the communications sector in order to be in a position to assess whether future changes would require adjustment to the regulatory approach. To that end, the ACCC indicated that it will monitor the development of new communications services and, should competition concerns arise in relation to the provision of these services, it would address these concerns in the first instance using specific communications and general competition law provisions in the CCA.[8]

Finally, the ACCC noted that enhanced consumer access to data presents an opportunity for enhanced consumer participation and will help unlock better consumer decision making in purchases. It should also enable service providers to tailor products to consumer needs and make switching between services easier for consumers. These changes are expected to drive greater competition between service providers. In May 2018 the Australian Government approved a new "consumer data right" (CDR) regime, to be overseen by the ACCC.[9] The CDR Rules were introduced for the banking sector in February 2020. The Rules provide the foundational framework for how the CDR operates in the banking sector and the ACCC will make sector specific rules for each new sector that is covered by the CDR.[10] It is currently consulting on a rules framework in the energy sector[11] with further sectors to follow. The government is yet to announce which sector, including potentially telecommunications, will be next.

Results, impact and lessons learnt

The ACCC's market study has not found a need to significantly alter the regulatory framework or approach to the communications sector, finding that it remains fit for purpose despite significant technological change and disruption. A key driver of this finding is that the ACCC has a comprehensive and flexible set of regulatory tools at its disposal.

However, the ACCC has made the following observations about regulation of the sector in the coming years:

- Newer communications services are likely to require less *ex ante* regulation than legacy ones as they are not characterised by the natural monopoly characteristics of traditional communications services/because of the dynamic and often more competitive conditions in which they are emerging. Where appropriate, sector-specific and general anti-competitive conduct provisions will be applied.

- Some newer services may emerge as recognised competitors to existing services (e.g. the emergence of fixed wireless as a competitor to fixed line broadband). Where this occurs the need for vertical separation regulation will be considered based on the relative market power of the firms within the sector. However, where the emerging service represents an increase to competition the appropriate change to regulation may be to remove some regulation on the incumbent provider.

- In this fast changing environment, there is a need to be vigilant and for regulators to remain informed of market developments, particularly as technological changes can occur very quickly meaning that problems can arise equally as quickly. To this end, the ACCC is focusing on some additional information gathering and monitoring efforts in the sector, particularly on emerging markets such as the IoT and discrete markets for NBN transmission services.

- Consumer access to data presents an opportunity for enhanced consumer participation and will help unlock better consumer decision making in purchases. It should also enable service providers to tailor products to consumer needs and make switching between services easier for consumers.

These changes are expected to drive greater competition between service providers. In 2018 the Australian Government initiated this right by introducing the CDR in the banking sector.

Co-operation

The Australian Communications and Media Authority (ACMA) is the authority responsible for regulating broadcasting, radio communications, telecommunications and the internet. The ACMA and ACCC's functions largely complement each other, with some overlap in relation to consumer safeguards. The ACCC provides advice to the ACMA on competition issues regarding spectrum allocation processes including recommendations on allocation limits on request. The ACCC also provides submissions to ACMA public consultation processes where relevant, and meets regularly with ACMA at a staff level on matters of mutual interest.

The ACCC and ACMA have established a Memorandum of Understanding to govern their relationship to provide for effective co-operation to contribute to both bodies effectively and efficiently discharging their functions. This includes the sharing of information and cross-appointment arrangements. These arrangements provide for both regulators to provide timely and expert input into each other's decision-making processes. The close relationship between the two agencies has been particularly important in developing strategies to address consumer issues that have arisen during the migration of consumers from legacy networks to the NBN. Both agencies have put in place complementary regulations to address gaps and failures in the migration process.

The ACCC ensured that the ACMA was engaged and consulted during critical junctures of the market study, including through the sharing of draft reports and discussion papers and the industry forum held mid-way through the study.

In terms of international co-operation, the ACCC participates in a number of international forums and interacts with international counterparts through these fora. It also has a range of arrangements with specific international counterparts relating to a range of functions. The ACCC engages regularly on communications matters with its New Zealand counterpart, the New Zealand Commerce Commission. Meetings with the United Kingdom regulator, Ofcom and the United States' Federal Communications Commission occur more sporadically on issues of mutual interest.

Notes

[1] ACCC, Communications Sector Market Study Final Report, April 2018, pp.16-18, https://www.accc.gov.au/publications/digital-platforms-inquiry-final-report.

Note: The ACCC also conducted an inquiry into Digital Platforms in 2018-19 that was separate to the Communications Market Study. The findings of the Digital Platforms Inquiry can be found at https://www.accc.gov.au/publications/digital-platforms-inquiry-final-report.

[2] For more information please see: https://www.accc.gov.au/focus-areas/market-studies/communications-sector-market-study.

[3] ACCC, Communications Sector Market Study Final Report, April 2018, pp.13, https://www.accc.gov.au/publications/digital-platforms-inquiry-final-report.

[4] Ibid, p. 155.

[5] Telecommunications Legislation Amendment (Competition and Consumer Safeguards) Bill 2010: https://www.legislation.gov.au/Details/C2010B00242/Explanatory%20Memorandum/Text.

[6] Ibid.

[7] Ibid, p.155.

[8] Ibid.

[9] Australian Government, Consumer Data right website, https://treasury.gov.au/consumer-data-right.

[10] For more information on the CDR regime and the ACCC's role see: https://www.accc.gov.au/focus-areas/consumer-data-right-cdr-0.

[11] ACCC, CDR in the Energy Sector, https://www.accc.gov.au/focus-areas/consumer-data-right-cdr/energy-cdr/energy-rules-framework-consultation.

Adapting to significant change through growth in functions and resourcing: Case study on the Australian Energy Regulator (AER)

Context

The role and detailed work of any regulator is inevitably shaped by developments in the markets it regulates. In energy, the market is in transition, with significant technological, behavioural and systemic change underway at all levels, and so the Australian Energy Regulator (AER) has to evolve and grow to meet new challenges.

Recognising the importance to the economy of a properly resourced regulator, and following an external consultants' review commissioned by government along with the findings of a review into the future security of the National Electricity Market undertaken by Australia's Chief Scientist Dr Alan Finkel, both of which found a case for enhanced resources, the Australian Government in 2017 significantly increased the AER's budget and headcount. Over the following two years, its staffing rose by almost 75%. It was also given new responsibilities, with the new resources for example enabling fresh work developing a mechanism for a default market offer, putting a value on reliability and ongoing reform in the regulation of gas networks.

The AER decided to grow in a careful and considered way, recognising that bringing in the right skills and expertise, and properly scoping and engaging on new projects, would be vital to long-term success for the regulator.

As a first step it committed to expanding existing teams to improve timeliness and apply resources to areas where its effectiveness had been constrained in the past. Following this, the AER decided to build key capabilities that it had previously been unable to establish fully.

Alongside this, the AER published its first Strategic Statement in August 2017, and it knew it needed to make changes to give practical effect to this significant document. It sets out the regulator's purpose as working to make all Australian energy consumers better off, now and in the future, and it includes five strategic objectives.

To embed the Strategic Statement, deliver its new responsibilities and make the most of its new funding, the AER established an ambitious program, with a series of work streams, to change how it operates. This ranged from its structure and workforce, to governance, culture and ways of working.

Issues

Adapting to significant change: growth in functions and resourcing

The AER's most recent stakeholder survey[1] found that 79% were satisfied with how effectively the AER performed its functions as a regulator (slightly up on 2016), with only 5% dissatisfied. Eighty seven percent said that the AER was trustworthy, and 81% said it had a clear direction and purpose. However, it always knew it could do more if it had more resources. In 2017, following a consultants' report and a major review of the future security of the National Electricity Market, the government recognised this with a significant funding boost and an expansion of the AER's roles and responsibilities.

This meant the AER could grow its teams, building on its existing cohort of talented and motivated individuals, and open up opportunities for development and capacity in areas that had previously been under-resourced. But while this was an exciting opportunity, it came with challenges too:

- The major growth in the organisation meant the AER would have to find entirely new ways of working.
- Its organisation had not just become bigger but also broader, with a much wider range of responsibilities.
- It had a very diverse staffing mix, with one-quarter of staff (and half of its senior people) having been in the organisation for more than a decade and so used to working in a particular way, and one-quarter being with the AER for less than a year.
- The organisation was already extremely busy, with more functions being added, but the process of change would itself demand more time and effort from staff.
- The context the AER was working in was not static – with an increase in functions and resourcing even as its review and restructure were underway.
- The change process was taking place against a backdrop of unparalleled political and public interest in the energy sector.

Community expectations of what a regulator does have altered and the AER had to adapt. It was a long way from the stereotype of an expert, economic regulator sitting alone making highly technical decisions. It had to understand consumer attitudes, experiences and needs, work in an open way, and move beyond consultation to true engagement. In addition, it had to collaborate with all its stakeholders while maintaining its independence.

Approach and intervention

The AER's Strategic Transformation Program

The AER commissioned external consultant, Nous Group, to work with it on identifying the skills and expertise most needed to deliver for consumers, and how best to structure the larger organisation to accommodate new functions and deliver on its broadened remit. This was framed by the Strategic Statement and a series of discussions about what a high-performing regulator looks like.

Nous ran an extensive program with staff, senior management and Board members – there were for example around half a dozen all-day sessions with the SMT and Board throughout the life of the project. This process considered the current state of the organisation, what it could be like in future, likely external challenges, desired ways of working and priorities in terms of new capabilities. This resulted in a discussion paper with Nous's initial analysis and conclusions, which formed the basis for further staff engagement. Nous then produced a further, final paper setting out its recommendations for change. These centred on three key areas:

- Governance – regulatory and operational decision making
- Organisation structure
- Workforce priorities.

Following further discussion, the AER's Strategic Transformation Program, which had been established alongside the Nous review, translated the recommendations into a detailed plan of action, which ran throughout 2018 and 2019. The AER decided to focus first on introducing important new capabilities, making structural changes to enable this. It adopted all of the Nous proposals on structure, with a few relatively minor changes, then moved onto governance and ways of working changes.

While maintaining critical functions the AER decided to establish new or enhanced capabilities in strategic communication, policy development and influence, consumer insight and engagement, and compliance and enforcement. It also decided to embed an ongoing change function in the structure, so that its Strategic Transformation Program (the Program) was not simply a one-off.

This led to a very different structure for the AER, which became operational in July 2018. It moved from five to eight branches, each led by a General Manager reporting to the CEO:

- Policy and Performance – to help the AER develop its insight and perspectives on key energy and regulatory issues, and provide analytical services to the whole organisation and support how it develops as an organisation.
- Strategic Communication and Corporate Services – to manage the AER's communications and relationships, and ensures it has the services it needs to support its work.
- Compliance and Enforcement – to develop and implement a strategic, risk-based approach to compliance, so that all regulated businesses meet their obligations.
- Consumers and Markets – to provide challenge on consumer issues, expertise on consumer engagement and insight, retail market consumer protection, and regulation of emerging business models.
- Market Performance – to monitor and report on retail and wholesale businesses' performance and lead an organisation-wide approach to data systems.
- Distribution – to lead the AER's strategy in relation to electricity distribution businesses, including delivery of network revenue determinations (resets).
- Transmission and Gas – to lead its strategy in relation to transmission and gas businesses, including delivery of resets.
- Networks Finance and Reporting – to support the Distribution and Transmission teams with specialist finance and modelling expertise, and lead on network performance reporting.

The AER then undertook significant recruitment, with a series of recruitment rounds in 2018 and 2019. This was a chance both to bring new people into the organisation and promote existing colleagues, but was in itself a significant amount of work.

Alongside this the AER initiated several important pieces of work on governance and ways of working:

- It created new operational priorities, to provide a bridge between its high-level Strategic Statement and detailed project planning. It also created new policy priorities.
- It developed new approaches to portfolio management, along with enhanced risk management and business planning processes.
- It put in place regular reporting to its Senior Management Team (SMT) and Board through a new organisational health and performance dashboard.
- It undertook a major review of its compliance and enforcement work, with a new Compliance & Enforcement policy and priorities supported by different ways of working.

Results, impact and lessons learnt

Through the Program the AER made some significant changes to the organisation, establishing new functions, structures and ways of working. Having periodically reviewed the effectiveness of the changes, the view of senior staff and Board was that together these changes have made the AER a more effective organisation.

The AER recognised in the design of the program it needed to support its wider leadership team to play a key role in the change process. Over the course of a year, it ran an extensive leadership program, "Leading through change", delivered by external consultants. The leadership program comprises all-SMT workshops, one-to-one coaching with each General Manager, group workshops with directors, facilitated sessions with each branch's senior leadership team, and all-staff sessions in selected new branches. It aimed both to establish effective leadership teams at senior management and branch level, and develop the change skills of individual leaders.

As the AER took on new functions and started to work differently, it was cognisant of the major impact this type of change could have on its people. The senior management team has had a strong focus on staff wellbeing. Amongst other things, a new People, Culture and Wellbeing Committee was set up, with representation from across the organisation. It developed practical initiatives to support a positive culture in the AER, as well as acting as a bridge between staff and management for effective feedback and identification of any emerging issues.

Other lessons learnt include:

- The Program did not proceed at the planned pace, largely because its scope broadened considerably. The AER did not for example initially know when or if the Board would be likely to increase in size and experience a major change in membership. The Program operated flexibly to accommodate this.

- Similarly, significant new functions and resources were added by government while the program was underway, so the planned structure and capabilities had to allow for some flexibility.

- The pressure of substantive work meant the AER had historically underinvested in corporate functions in the organisation, and although the new structure aimed to remedy this, the change process itself was run on a tight budget.

- Staff adapted well to the new structure and were keen to see some of the new ways of working put in place. They were heavily engaged in the early stages of the Program but this faded somewhat and the AER had to refresh the Program's internal profile as it undertook further work in 2019.

- A highly experienced and close-knit leadership team, which understood its own need for change and embraced new colleagues from outside the organisation, was a key success factor for the Program.

Postscript

This case study was written in early 2019, and presented by the AER Board member Cristina Cifuentes at the OECD Network of Economic Regulators event. But as noted above, the change process is never one with a defined end point, and much has happened since then.

The Strategic Transformation Program was concluded as a discrete programme of work at the end of 2019. A new Chair, Clare Savage, joined the organisation in September 2019, and following legislative change the Board expanded to five members in early 2020, four of whom were new – Catriona Lowe, Justin Oliver and Eric Groom, along with Clare. Jim Cox was appointed Deputy Chair. Cristina herself stepped down from her AER Board role as part of this process. A new CEO, Liz Develin, joined in May 2020.

The Board has established four committees, covering Markets, Networks, Enforcement & Compliance, and Policy & Governance. Further changes are being made to ways of working, and there is likely to be further structural change. The Board has initiated a new strategy process, which will result in the creation of a Strategic Plan.

In short, the AER's transformation process is evolving and renewing itself in the face of new challenges.

Note

[1] AER Stakeholder Survey 2018, https://www.aer.gov.au/publications/corporate-documents/aer-stakeholder-survey-2018.

Using new technologies to map transport flows in Brazil: Case study on the National Land Transportation Regulatory Agency (ANTT)

Context

The competencies of the Brazil's National Land Transportation Agency (*Agência Nacional de Transportes Terrestres,* ANTT) are:

* granting, inspecting and managing the contract of concessionaires of road and railway infrastructure.
* providing permits and licenses, inspecting and managing the contracts (when a permit has been granted) of the interstate and international transportation of passengers, by bus and train.
* registering road freight transportation companies, truckers and trucks; defining and inspecting the minimum rate of road freight transportation in Brazil (new law[1] issued in 2018 after Brazilian general strike of truckers).

Inspections are mandatory for all sectors regulated by ANTT. Concerning the road transportation services of goods and passengers, one single ANTT department holds the inspections, the "Inspections Superintendency".

Issues

Inspecting transportation services is difficult and costly due to the size of the country. ANTT does not have enough human resources to cover all the country, although ANTT has approximately 2,400 collaborators throughout Brazil. As an example, due to a lack of personnel, ANTT is not undertaking any inspections concerning the minimum rate of freight transportation services. Indeed, the Brazilian Government did not anticipate the necessity of issuing a new legislation and did not guarantee adequate financial resources through allocated budget. In this sense, the use of technology is deemed necessary to maintain the Agency's proper functioning.

A fiscal document must be emitted for each transportation operation that involves a payment. Since when the transporter is not transporting goods or when the goods are owned by the transporter there is no need to have a registration at ANTT, not having access to the fiscal documents prevented the agency to efficiently target the enforcement actions for those who are being paid to transport goods, or to make the best use of its scarce human resources.

Approach and intervention

ANTT initiated a program called "Green Channel Brazil" (*Canal Verde Brasil*), an intelligent national network for the perception, monitoring and mapping of transport flows in logistics corridors. This system aims at producing data, information and evidence to inform market regulation, national logistics planning, and economic and financial indicators.

The initiative arose four years ago from the identified need to enforce regulatory compliance of freight and passenger transportation in a 1.7 million kilometer highway network. As of today, ANTT has less than 500 agents monitoring regulation enforcement and the number of agents dedicated to enforcement had been reduced at the time. Aiming to decrease the interference of different entities enforcement actions at the transportation sector, which increased the transportation costs, and seizing the opportunity of the recent creation of electronic fiscal documents, the Agency employees developed the program. They submitted it to higher instances of the Brazilian Public Administration without much resistance for approval to guarantee the necessary funds to the project. At that time, many Brazilian Government entities were submitting projects based on technology to amplify their capabilities. With the funds guaranteed, ANTT conducted a bidding process to choose the company that would provide de service of installing and maintaining the infrastructure of the portals and transmitting the data.

Both an optical character recognition camera and an antenna that identifies radio frequency registers that the vehicle passes through the electronic reading point. The use of several identification methods provide enhanced precision as license plates are not always readable nor are the electronic chips always reliable. The vehicle's identification data, transit timing and geo-referenced location of the electronic reading point are then cross-checked with information registered in other databases of Government and State agencies, to check regulatory compliance.

Figure 2.1. Green Channel Brazil: traffic tracking

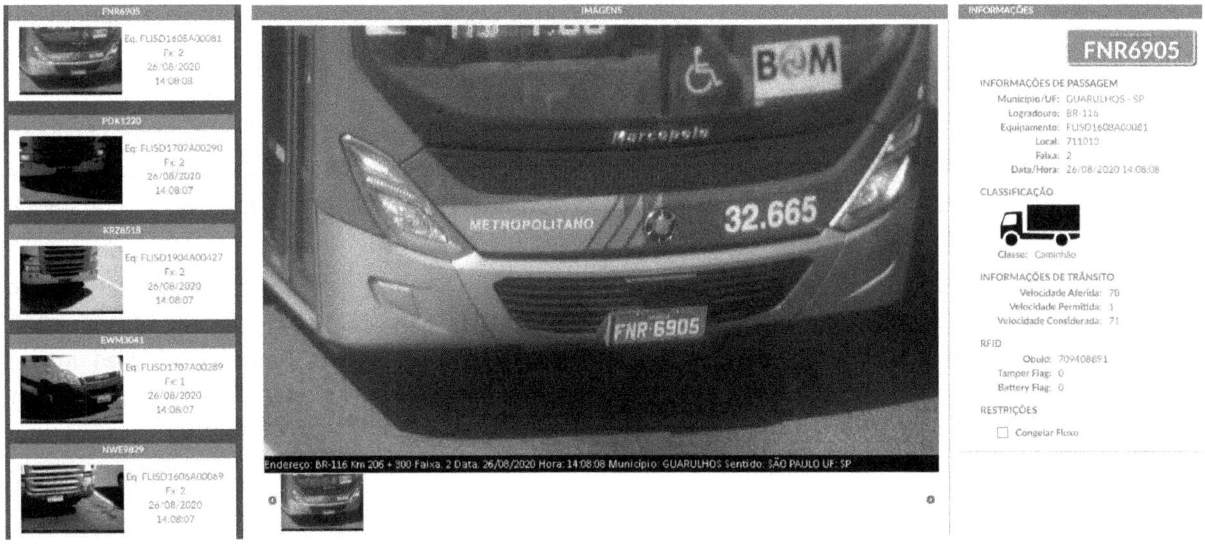

Source: Information provided by ANTT, 2019.

Results, impact and lessons learnt

The advantages of the "Green Channel Brazil" project are:

- reduction of the logistics costs resulting from the controls on transportation
- de-bureaucratisation of the state apparatus
- increased competitiveness of the national product
- reductions in public funding and investments in analogical control processes and unification of the controls in a single moment, that is, when the vehicle passes through the electronic reading points

- increased control over transportation operations
- increased safety
- generation of information and knowledge for the improvement of the cost and benefit analysis of the regulatory activity of the markets, for planning public policies and investments in the transportation and logistics sectors.

In a phrase, the main advantage of the "Green Channel Brazil" programme is the reduction of the costs of production, transportation and exportation of Brazilian goods. The initiative decreases government costs through sharing data and information with other government agencies.

Thanks to this system, the geographic location of the trucks and their probable time of arrival to the ports can be tracked through approximately 55 portals installed in different roads.

ANTT has already co-ordinated with Santos Port Authority to integrate the network system within the Port Without Paper (*Porto Sem Papel*) system. Until recently, there was no scheduling system to organise the trucks arrivals to the port. In 2014, the port authority created the requirement to preschedule deliveries. However, in the absence of serious enforcement freight transportation companies did not respect this requirement. In 2014 and 2015, ANTT agents enforced prescheduling by stopping trucks on the highways and requiring truckers to make the appointment before reaching the port, reducing the percentage of unscheduled deliveries to 13%. Since 2016, the *Canal Verde Brasil* program has been monitoring and enforcing prescheduling of cargo deliveries in co-ordination with the Port Authority. As a result, only 7% of the vehicles get to the port without a prescheduled time window for unloading of cargo (100% before the implementation of the program). The program allowed to put an end to massive traffic jams and delays of cargo delivery. This initiative has translated into a reduction of waiting time for trucks that disembark at the Port of Santos. The estimated loss cost due to congestion in the Port of Santos was BRL 115 million per year before the system implementation.

The connection of the network system with the São Paulo State Treasury Office (verification of goods information transported) helped to achieve a 6% increase in the collection of the value-added tax on sales and services for the São Paulo State over the year 2018 by detecting vehicles that are traveling constantly without an associated fiscal document.

At this stage, the major result of the program for ANTT is that the freight transportation inspection went from 905 213 vehicles inspected between 2010 and 2016, to 116 million vehicles inspected between 2016 and January 2020. In addition, the system also allowed ANTT to inspect irregular vehicles in the transportation of passengers by bus. ANTT intends to increase the use of the system to inspect passenger transportation, which depends on an internal improvement on database interoperability.

Co-operation

The intelligent national network began within ANTT, but its integration with other governmental bodies is crucial. ANTT has already implemented co-ordination concerning entities in the sectors of transportation and transportation regulation, fiscal, justice, agriculture and planning. ANTT usually formalises the co-operation is through a Technical Cooperation Agreement and the co-operation is implemented by the creation and granting of access to webservices by the involved entities. Usually, the agency organises a pilot project of the co-operation to help stablish the technical characteristics of the Cooperation Agreement. The main difficulties in expanding the system and increasing co-ordination with other entities are the budgetary restrictions and the lack of systems in other entities or interoperability issues.

Regarding port entities ANTT has an agreement in force with the Santos Port Authority and aims to help decrease Brazil's cost of transportation in other ports, enforcing the need of scheduling deliveries and informing the ports of the vehicles moving towards the facilities. ANTT will benefit by the limitation of access to the ports only to registered vehicles, a measure that enforces the need of registration at the agency.

The co-operation with the National Transportation Infrastructure Department (Dnit) and the Regulatory Agency of the State of São Paulo (Artesp) allowed ANTT to install portals at highways not regulated by the agency (2 portals in co-operation with Artesp and 8 with Dnit). The access to the data of Canal Verde Brasil allows Dnit to make better use of its resources. Having access to the traffic volume at the portals, they can avoid paying for surveys when planning the construction of new highways or an intervention at the highways under their responsibility. Artesp is a strategic regulatory agency because of the traffic volume at the State of São Paulo. One studied future use of the data exchange between the regulatory agencies is to prevent toll avoidance. One example is at the beltway of São Paulo. Sometimes vehicles enter the city to avoid paying tolls. With the information exchange Artesp will know the planned deliveries of the vehicle and, consequently, if the vehicle has a planned delivery to the city or if it is avoiding the toll payment.

ANTT gives access to its data on demand to the Federal Road Police and the Ministry of Justice. The access to the list of vehicles that crossed the portals and of passengers transported in services regulated by the agency enables these entities to locate passengers or vehicles that may have problems with the justice system. With the data exchange ANTT can help them locate, for example, stolen vehicles or fugitives. The co-operation with the Ministry of Justice will guarantee free access to the database of the existing vehicles in Brazil. Without the co-operation the access is paid each time the database is consulted.

The Fiscal Entities are of crucial importance since they allow ANTT to have access to the data of those who are providing goods freight service. Every state of Brazil has its own fiscal department, which makes the task more difficult. The state of Rio Grande do Sul, however, is responsible for storing the data of all State Fiscal authorities. Due to legal restraints, ANTT could access only the data of companies that had previously authorised the agency to do so. Hence, until October of 2019, ANTT had access to the data of only 60% of the fleet. Due to a new rule ANTT does not need to have the transporter's permission to access their data. As a result, the Agency expects an increase of its capacity of enforcing freight transportation.

Note

[1] Provisional Measure No. 832/2018, converted in Bill No. 13.703, of 8 August 2018, that creates the National Minimum Rate for Land Freight Transportation Services Policy.

Lessons from the Regulatory Modernisation Initiative: Case study on the Canadian Transportation Agency (CTA)

Over the past two decades, transportation sectors have been undergoing rapid change in business models and operating practices as a result of factors such as technological advancements and market liberalisation. At the same time, users' (the travelling public and shippers) expectations with regard to transportation services have increased. It is important to ensure that transportation regulators have the appropriate mandates, authorities, and tools to keep up with these changes. The Canadian Transportation Agency's (CTA) Regulatory Modernization Initiative (RMI) was aimed at addressing regulatory issues related to these rapidly evolving standards, practices and technologies. The CTA also leverages co-operative relationships with other federal organisations and international counterparts to address issues where regulatory jurisdictions may overlap.

The CTA is an independent regulator and quasi-judicial tribunal that, among other things, makes, applies, and enforces economic and accessibility-related regulations covering Canada's national transportation system. Most of those regulations were decades-old and, in some respects, outdated, which had problematic implications for industry, travellers and shippers, and the efficiency and effectiveness of the CTA itself. To address this regulatory sclerosis, the CTA launched its RMI in May 2016 – an ambitious project to review and update every regulation the CTA administers, with the goal of ensuring that the regulations keep pace with changes in business models, user expectations, disruptive technologies and best practices in the regulatory field.

This case study describes how the RMI unfolded, draws some lessons on the challenges and factors for success associated with such an initiative, and underscores the importance of both regular reviews of legal frameworks and greater multilateral co-operation to address emerging issues.

Context

The CTA exercises oversight in respect of economic and accessibility matters for Canada's federally-regulated modes of transportation: air, interprovincial and international rail, inter-provincial and international marine, and (with respect to accessibility) inter-provincial bus services.

The CTA has three core mandates:

- Ensuring that the national transportation system runs efficiently and smoothly in the interests of all Canadians: those who work and invest in it; the producers, shippers, travellers and businesses who rely on it; and the communities where it operates
- Protecting the human right of persons with disabilities to an accessible transportation network
- Providing consumer protection for air passengers.

To deliver these mandates, the CTA has three primary tools at its disposal:

- The first is rule-making: The CTA develops and applies ground rules that establish the rights and responsibilities of transportation service providers and users, and that level the playing field among competitors. These rules – which can take the form of binding regulations or less formal guidelines, codes of practice, or interpretation notes – are applied by the CTA through the issuance of regulatory authorities, licences and permits, and through a dedicated compliance monitoring and enforcement program.

- The second tool is dispute resolution: the CTA, on application, resolves disputes that arise between transportation service providers on the one hand, and their clients and neighbours on the other, using a range of tools from facilitation and mediation to arbitration and adjudication. When it delivers adjudications, the CTA acts as a quasi-judicial tribunal and exercises all the powers of a superior court.

- Finally, the CTA provides information on the transportation system, including the rights and responsibilities of transportation service providers and users, and the CTA's own mandates and services.

Issues

Many of the regulations for which the CTA is responsible came into force 20 to 25 years ago. In many cases, the provisions of these regulations did not keep pace with changes in business models, user expectations, and best practices in the regulatory field.

As a result, transportation service providers had to comply with sometimes cumbersome administrative obligations, protections for travellers (including those with disabilities) were uneven, and the CTA's ability to deliver timely and appropriate services was affected.

In respect of accessibility, prior to the RMI, there existed only two sets of regulations: one that set out certain accessibility-related service obligations for airlines, and the other prescribing mandatory training for front-line employees who assist persons with disabilities moving through the federally-regulated transportation network. To fill the gaps not covered by these regulations, the CTA developed six voluntary codes on accessibility matters. As they were not formal regulations, these codes were not legally binding.

In respect of consumer protection for air passengers, the previous regime in Canada only required that each airline develop and apply a tariff – a document outlining the carrier's terms and conditions of carriage. The CTA's only role was to determine whether an airline had properly applied its tariff and whether the terms in the tariff were reasonable. As each airline develops its own tariff, it was difficult for air travellers to know what rights and recourses were available to them. Other jurisdictions, notably the EU and the U.S., had developed more general air passenger rights regimes that laid out minimum standards of treatment and levels of compensation for flight disruptions.

In respect of market entry and operating conditions for air carriers, previous regulations included elements such as lengthy application periods and CTA approval requirements for routine activities, both of which were out-of-step with how the industry had evolved. They also set minimum insurance levels whose real value had been seriously eroded by inflation.

Finally, for rail transportation, previous regulations referenced statutes that had been repealed and did not reflect new obligations and processes created by legislative amendments.

Approach and intervention

The RMI was launched to address these challenges. It had four consultation phases: one each on accessible transportation, air transportation, air passenger protection, and rail transportation.

For accessible transportation, the RMI consolidated the existing regulations and the voluntary codes of practice into one comprehensive, robust, and binding set of regulations called the Accessible Transportation for Persons with Disabilities Regulations (ATPDR). They cover six key areas:

- Communications;

- training for transportation personnel that interact with persons with disabilities;
- services;
- technical requirements for facilities and equipment;
- requirements for terminals, and
- border and security screening.

While the new regulations address emerging issues not related to new technologies – such as accessible travel for persons with severe allergies – they do respond to the changing technological landscape. In particular, the regulations set accessibility requirements for technology and equipment now commonly used by transportation service providers and travellers, such as online check-in, self-service kiosks, and complex on-board entertainment systems. In keeping with the Canadian process, these regulations were pre-published for public comment, and the final regulations were published in summer 2019. The regulations, most of which will come into effect in June 2020, will benefit Canadians with or without disabilities who use the national transportation system.

In terms of the air passenger protection component of the RMI, the *Transportation Modernization Act* gave the CTA authority to make regulations establishing minimum airline obligations towards passengers in a number of areas, including clear communication, delayed or cancelled flights, denied boarding, tarmac delays over three hours, the seating of children under the age of 14, damaged or lost baggage, and the transportation of musical instruments. These new regulations have brought about a transparent, clear, fair, and consistent regime to the Canadian market, and align Canada with best practices in other international regulatory regimes such as the EU and the U.S. The Air Passenger Protection Regulations (APPR) were pre-published at the end of 2018 for public comment and finalised in May 2019. The requirements took effect in two phases – on 15 July 2019 and on 15 December 2019.

The other two phases of the RMI updated the CTA's existing air transportation and rail transportation regulations. These have not been updated frequently and as a result, they have not kept up with the significant changes in their respective industries. The objective for the air transportation phase was to amend the Air Transportation Regulations, which set out the criteria that air carriers must meet regarding the carriage of passengers and/or cargo by air, to better reflect market realities (e.g., amending insurance coverage requirements that were unchanged for three decades). Amendments to the CTA's Rail Regulations included filing requirements for railway insurance, penalties for non-compliance with railway requirements, and updates to the regulations to reflect statutory changes in recent years. The amended air and rail regulations were finalised and published in summer 2019. Building on the momentum of the RMI, the CTA is looking at further regulatory reforms. In December 2019, the CTA launched public consultations on a second phase of regulatory reform in the area of accessible transportation. Areas of focus for these consultations include how to apply the ATPDR to small transportation providers, and what to require of transportation providers with respect to emotional support animals (ESAs) and service animals other than dogs. The CTA is also looking at additional updates to the rail regulations it administers.

Results, impacts and lessons learnt

As the ATPDR are not yet in force and the APPR only completely came into force at the end of 2019, it may take time to assess the impacts of the new regulations on the Canadian transportation network, and how effectively they have aided the CTA in pursuing its mandates. A regulatory cost benefit analysis (CBA) for the accessibility regulations, the ATPDR, suggested a cost to industry of CAD 7 million per year over a 10 year period, with benefits to Canadians of CAD 80 million per year over the same period. Qualitative impacts included reduced stigmatic harm, increased safety, and greater independence for persons with disabilities and wider access to desired destinations. For the air passenger regulations, the APPR, the regulatory CBA suggested a cost of CAD 218 million per year over a 10-year period for air carriers, with benefits to Canadians of CAD 232 million per year over the same period.

The consultations undertaken as part of the RMI also identified constraints in regulating at the national level that do not permit the CTA to fully respond to emerging technologies that disrupt the air industry, or air industry issues of an international nature. One example is the practice of data scraping air carriers' websites to obtain the lowest possible fare for customers. This practice involves extracting pricing and flight scheduling data to monitor and analyse trends in order to combine several unrelated itineraries, or to take advantage of "throwaway ticketing" to present the cheapest itinerary to the end user. Such websites circumvent Canadian regulatory requirements on airfare pricing advertising as they typically operate outside of Canada. The impacts of disruptive technologies on air travel is an issue that implicates different sectors, as well as different jurisdictions within Canada and internationally. Engagement with other federal organisations and other levels of government in Canada, other states, and international organisations such as the International Civil Aviation Organization (ICAO) will be required to assess the breadth of this issue and address it as required.

International co-operation is also key to addressing technological challenges in promoting accessibility across jurisdictions. For instance, as mobility aids become larger and more customised, more work is needed within and across countries to co-ordinate their carriage, particularly on airlines. The CTA decided to address this issue by creating a multi-stakeholder Mobility Aids Forum that collaborated to develop near-term goals and recommendations to promote the safe storage and transportation of mobility aids. The CTA is also working to promote accessibility more broadly at the international level. In particular, the CTA has joined with other federal organisations to increase the emphasis placed on accessible air transportation in ICAO deliberations. The CTA and other representatives from participating states are also leveraging new data sharing technologies to create an easily accessible compendium of regulations, statutes, and policies to promote a harmonised approach for accessible international travel. One key objective of this initiative is the passage of an accessibility-related resolution. These efforts recognise that when travel crosses borders, solving problems requires international support and co-ordination leading to international solutions.

Co-operation

The CTA actively fosters co-operative relationships with other organisations, both nationally and internationally, in order to share information and best practices, align regulations, and adopt and promote international standards.

The CTA has established formal arrangements with other jurisdictions and regularly participates in international fora. This has included:

- Establishing a dozen Memoranda of Understanding (MOU) with other Canadian federal regulators as well as federal regulators in the U.S. and Mexico to foster co-operation and facilitate the sharing of information and best practices. The MOUs, among other things, allow for the sharing of information and data related to transportation and dispute resolution.

- Collaborating with international counterparts through fora such as ICAO in order to promote uniform policy and regulatory practices across the air industry.

- Regularly participating in the OECD's NER conferences and initiatives. This forum allows the CTA to share its experiences and lessons learned to an international audience of economic regulators, and it also provides an opportunity for the CTA to learn from the international community.

International consultation and analysis of best practices are a critical component of the CTA's regulatory development process. In the case of the RMI, the CTA held meetings with counterparts in the United States and the EU to discuss the regulatory proposals, potential international considerations, and to learn about their experiences. Furthermore, when developing regulations at the federal level, government departments and agencies are required by the Treasury Board of Canada Secretariat to assess the approach of other jurisdictions in order to identify possibilities for regulatory alignment.

New approaches to regulating transport in Finland: Case study on the Transport and Communications Agency (TRAFICOM)

Context

The Finnish Transport and Communications Agency (*Liikenne-ja viestintävirasto,* TRAFICOM) is the national licensing and certification authority, as well as the registration and oversight authority in the field of transport and communications in Finland. TRAFICOM also issues technical and operational regulations complementing national legislation. TRAFICOM has as an objective to promote traffic safety and the smooth functioning of the transport system, and to ensure that everyone in Finland has access to high quality and secure communications connections and services. For TRAFICOM, the relevant transport market is very wide, encompassing driving license holders, car owners, sea captains, aerodromes, railway undertakings, etc.

Issues

For a very long time, different modes of transport have been regulated separately on all levels. At global level, there are the United Nations' framework for road transport, the International Civil Aviation Organization (ICAO) for aviation, the International Maritime Organization (IMO) for maritime issues and the Intergovernmental Organization for International Carriage by Rail (OTIF) for rail. The same separation continues regionally and most often also nationally. Yet, the approach to market regulation is very similar in all modes of transport: licensing and certification, registration, oversight, and passenger rights. In addition, the trends that initiate changes are the same: safety and security of the services, environmental challenges, digitalisation, automation, congestion in densely inhabited areas, etc.

Transport network is the backbone of societies. People and companies need transport services in their daily lives. The efficiency and sustainability of the transport services is an important time and cost factor for the industry as well as individuals. Often, end-users of transport services use combined services (travel chains). Companies delivering their products to the market may use road, rail, sea and/or air carriage; and people use their own car, bicycle or combinations of bus, metro, train, taxi travel, etc.

Finland has been an advocate and a spokesperson for the concept of "Mobility as a Service" (MAAS). The idea is to look at the transport system from the perspective of the end-users: What is, to the end-users, the easiest and most efficient way to access the transport services they need? How can they compare and combine different services, also taking into account the different motivations that guide their choices: time, cost, comfort, environmental values and so on?

Looking at the transport system as a whole, infrastructure matters a lot: the roads, the railways, the ports and waterways, as well as airports and airspace management. Additionally, the different services connected with transportation should be given particular attention: parking facilities, weather services, ticketing systems, etc.

Approach and intervention

The first step towards a transport system wide governance was the decision taken by the Finnish government to merge the different transport authorities. This decision led to the establishment in 2010 of two transport authorities:

- the Finnish Transport Safety Authority (Trafi), responsible for most licensing and certification tasks, transport registers, oversight and regulatory work in all modes of transport; and
- the Finnish Transport Agency, responsible for road, rail and water transport infrastructure and traffic management.

The significance of digitalisation, digital services and communication networks in transport became more and more evident. Therefore, when developing its organisational model, Trafi chose in 2012 a matrix model recognising the importance of data. Data was considered as the fifth mode of transport.

Figure 2.2. TRAFI organisational model

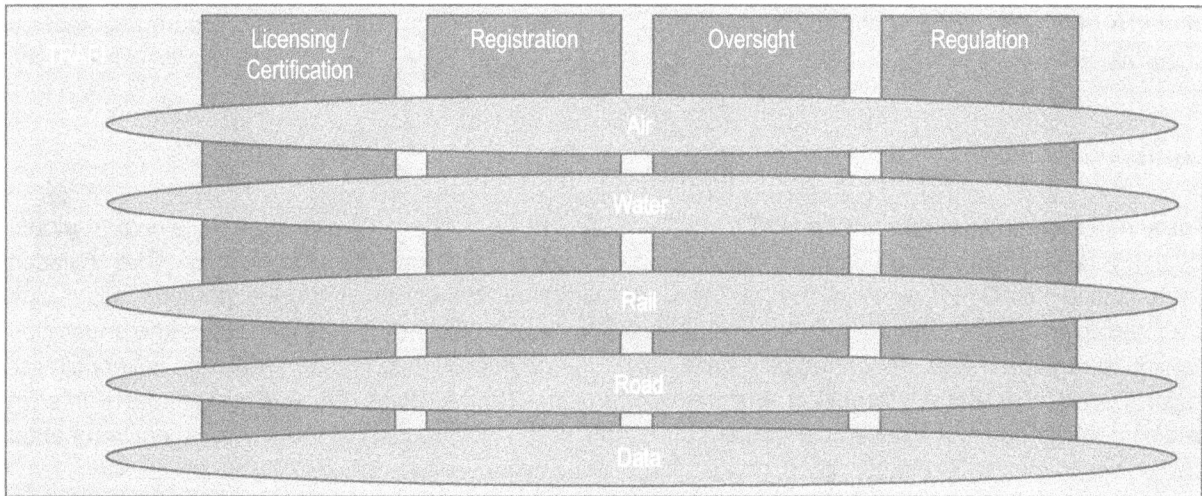

Source: information provided by TRAFICOM. 2019.

The most dramatic change, from the perspective of the personnel and of the customers, was to organise themselves according to the processes: one sector concentrating on oversight tasks, the second on certification and the third on registration, all covering all modes of transport. In addition, rule-making activities in different modes of transport were brought together. This change aimed at having experts from different modes of transport working side by side and learning from each other.

However, to maintain a transport mode oriented approach in such a process-oriented solution, directors general were nominated for all modes of transport, with their own staff. They were, in particular, responsible for international relations and relations with stakeholders, as well as making sure that all aspects of the authority responsibilities in their field were covered. As the role of data and digitalisation had also been recognised as an essential and overarching factor in all transportation, a director general for data issues was also nominated.

The challenge of this model was, however, the requirements it set for the "middle-management level". Heads of unit and other operative management level representatives had mostly experience from only one mode of transport. Consequently, they could not support and lead all experts in their unit, covering all modes of transport, in the same manner. From the perspective of customers, managers with a background in just one field, and yet responsible for activities in all modes of transport, lacked credibility, at least to a certain degree.

As a result, this process-based matrix organisation was after a while replaced with a "compromise" solution, which took into account the perspective of the customer, however, combining work in different modes of transport as much as possible.

The latest intervention in governance has been the establishment, in 2019, of the Finnish Transport and Communications Agency, or TRAFICOM, inheriting the tasks of Trafi, some of the tasks of the Finnish Transport Agency[1] and the tasks of the former Communications Agency.

The primary goals of this reform were to improve the ability to respond to the changes in customer needs and the operating environment, to develop and strengthen the strategic management of the administrative branch and to achieve synergy benefits. Another goal was to further improve the productivity and impact of administration through more versatile and effective use of resources. The reform aims at better use of transport-related data in the private sector and at generating new business activities. The objective is to better utilise the data for the benefit of the whole society. Also, digitalisation, service orientation in transport and creation of transport markets with the support of new legislation are bringing the transport and communications sectors closer together.

This merger was facilitated by the fact that the Finnish Ministry of Transport and Communications had already all these agencies under its umbrella. However, the agencies were different in size, which had naturally impacted the organisational cultures. Therefore, combining the agencies also meant e.g. that practicalities in the administrative "routines" needed to be fine-tuned. In addition, the duties of personnel engaged in overlapping tasks needed to be reviewed.

The objective of the new Agency is to promote traffic safety and the smooth functioning of the transport system, and to ensure that everyone in Finland has access to high quality and secure communications connections and services. With the involvement of the whole staff, TRAFICOM has been defining what kind of organisational culture it wants to have basing the work on its values: *trust, cooperation* and *capacity to change*. Promoting the environmental approach and the development of the transport system and market is looked at in networks that cross the organisation horizontally, including both management and expert level.

Also national transport legislation has undergone a major change: principle rules for transportation of passenger and goods in all modes of transport have been gathered in the same national law, the Transport Code or Transport Services Act. The main drivers for this amendment were digitalisation and deregulation. Some chapters of the Code deal only with one mode of transport, but several chapters cover all modes, regulating access to information on transport services, passenger rights, etc.

Results, impact and lessons learnt

Looking at the transport system as a whole has benefitted the Finnish Authorities. They have been able to learn from technological developments and best practices in different fields, and set up solutions that benefit the whole system. For example, a digital driver's licence has been developed, and the experience gained in that process is currently being used in projects preparing for digital pilots licences. Rules governing the collection and use of data relating to registration of vehicles, ships and aircraft, as well as personnel licences in different modes of transport where unified, which allows for better and more consistent service for customers, and facilitates work in the agency. Experts e.g. in data protection and cybersecurity are co-operating with all parts of the organisation, which gives them a wider view on developments in the sector.

To look for best practices and to take into account lessons learned in another domain is an approach that is visible in Finnish positions at international level, where issues having a wider impact are discussed: digitalisation, cybersecurity, automated vehicles, and environmental impacts of transport. The organisational changes in Finland have helped TRAFICOM in developing common approaches in many areas, such as transport registers, passengers' rights, medical practitioners' right and obligation to divulge information to the transport authority, etc.

Looking comprehensively at the transport system gives the Agency understanding on the differences between different modes of transport, as well as of the problems that these differences can create. Transport is a heavily regulated sector, where the basic rules are established at global level. Making changes requires work and agreement at global level.

Evidently, it is not easy to establish governance for such a wide field. To have a particular "cross-organisational" or horizontal approach to a particular phenomenon or common features of different systems, there are a variety of governance choices:

- You can establish a matrix organisation, where different dimensions are crossing each other (like in the picture on the previous page). The challenge of this approach is the management of resources (who decides on the use of resources, the priorities, and the budget).

- You can set cross-organisational teams. In a cross-organisational team, members dealing with similar issues are brought together from different parts of the organisation: they exchange information and best practices and can provide comprehensive analysis and reports. In Trafi and TRAFICOM, we have had for example the Dangerous Goods Team, discussing the developments and best practices in the transportation of dangerous goods. Another example is the Accessibility Team, where members look at different issues relating to accessibility of the transport system. The benefit of these teams is that they are often quite agile, and can react quickly to new tasks and responsibilities. The challenge of the team-model is management. When setting up a team it is therefore important to establish its tasks and describe how the team activities relate to the decision-making process.

- You can also set up special units to look at a particular feature of phenomenon. Such special units can support other parts of the organisation on a particular issue. For example, in TRAFICOM, we have a special unit dealing with experimentation and automation for the benefit of the whole transport system. We also have a common unit for transport information and analysis. The personnel working in such a special unit needs to actively co-operate with other parts of the organisation, in order to make an impact.

In summary, it can be said that there is no one governance model that would fit all purposes. In order to respond to market transformation and disruptive technologies, governmental agencies need to be agile, to review the appropriateness of their governance model regularly and have a variety of tools in their tool kit.

Note

[1] The Finnish Transport Agency was a government agency, responsibilities of which were split between TRAFICOM and the Ministry of Transport and Communication at the moment TRAFICOM was formed.

Developing data driven regulation for the digital ecosystem in France: Case study on the Electronic Communications, Postal and Print Media Distribution Regulatory Authority (ARCEP)

Context

France's Electronic Communications, Postal and Print Media Distribution Regulatory Authority (*Autorité de régulation des communications électroniques, des postes et de la distribution de la presse*, ARCEP) was created on 5 January 1997. At the time, the French Parliament gave ARCEP the task of shepherding the process of opening the electronic communications sector up to competition, and so enabling new operators to emerge alongside the incumbent carrier (France Telecom, since renamed Orange), and this for the benefit of end users.

The fixed and mobile calling and internet markets have evolved a great deal since then. Operators have deployed fixed (copper, fibre optic, etc.) and mobile (2G, 3G, 4G and now 5G) networks to provide not only telephone services but also internet access. These communication networks now play a vital role in the country's operation, and in the daily lives of the people of France. The market situation evolved considerably, as did the responsibilities of ARCEP, which were expanded to include, for instance, postal sector regulation in 2005, and the protection of net neutrality in 2015. ARCEP responsibilities were further expanded in 2016 with the Digital Republic Act and in 2019 via the Law on the modernisation of print media distribution, which reformed the "Bichet Act" and assigned the responsibility of regulating the print media sector to ARCEP. ARCEP's goal is now to ensure that private operators' growth trajectory and interests are reconciled with the objectives of achieving nationwide connectivity, and fair and effective competition between operators for the benefit of end users.

To meet these new challenges, ARCEP wanted to enter into a new and resolutely digital-centric cycle in its history: in 2015 it began a strategic review of its activities, entitled "ARCEP 360°". An open, transparent and participatory process that involved all of ARCEP's teams, as well as outside stakeholders.

At the end of process, ARCEP drew up a roadmap that defined the "causes to champion" in the coming years. It also adopted a mission statement, a brief text that seeks to define its fundamental *raison d'être*: "ARCEP is a neutral and expert arbitrator, architect and guardian of communications networks in France."

Issues

In 2015, ARCEP identified that end-users did not have a sufficient role in the regulatory process that would provide them the full ability to drive competition, innovation and investment.

A study commissioned by ARCEP in 2016 revealed that information such as quality of service, coverage, etc. was considered a key driver of choice by end-users and as a crucial element of analysis for collectivities. The study further showed that these stakeholders considered that this information was neither available nor understandable enough to make informed decisions.

One of the main triggers that pushed ARCEP to take action was the heterogeneity of mobile coverage among operators. This take leaded to a willingness to create the right incentives for operators to invest.

Another illustration is the fact that users and collectivities volunteered to collaborate with the regulator and take a role in the regulation but could not find the good entry points and tools to do it, generating a frustration for them and a lack of information for the regulator.

Approach and intervention

In order to answer to these issues, ARCEP chose to develop an approach of data-driven regulation. This approach is willing to be holistic and to deploy a new form of action that comes to complete the regulator's traditional toolkit.

The guiding principle is to harness the power of information to steer the market in the right direction.

One sort of action consists in refining the regulation tools to get able to analyse more information, on a finer level, and to detect weak signals or systemic problems in order to accelerate the regulation process and make it more efficient.

This being done, the second sort of action consists in giving more power to end-users and relay actors (public actors, associations, civil society, start-ups, etc.) with a more precise and personalised information. For example end-users have a strong power on the market, the power to "vote with their feet" and through their choices "reward" or "punish" actors on the market. Regulator can play an important role to help users to realise this potential and accompany users' choices in order to give good incentives on the market. This approach is inspired by the philosophy of nudge promoted by Richard Thaler, the winner of the 2017 Nobel Prize of economy.

This approach asks for a change of culture in the public sector. Adopting a "state as a platform" philosophy involves acknowledging that State has not the monopoly of general interest, every user, every actor can take its part of the defence of general interest and every citizen is placed in situation of playing a role in the regulation. Moreover, the state is not always the most relevant actor to better give information to users and it may be more efficient to act in a logic of empowerment of a RegTech ecosystem.

Since 2017, three main action plans have been developed by ARCEP teams in bringing regulating with data to life:

- First, the publication of maps which provide the user with a detailed comparison of telecom network coverage and quality of service across France.
- Then, the launch of a reporting platform named "*J'alerte l'ARCEP*" that gives everybody the power to report a malfunction in their relationship with their operator.
- Finally, the roll out of "Ma connexion Internet" a cartographic search engine providing end users with internet access technologies availability where they live

Regarding the publication of maps and search engines

This tool is very important to help users and all actors to have an easier and a better understanding of coverage and quality of telecom services in France: the idea was to convert pdf reports with nationally aggregated data into dynamic maps with locally detailed information. Doing so, ARCEP enriched the information presented to make it reflect better the daily experience of users and such, make them more able to compare and choose operators. Three tools were published until now:

The website "Monreseaumobile.fr" presents on the same page coverage 1) maps built by operators on four levels representing users experience; and 2) quality of service measures realised by ARCEP on the transport networks and in living places. This data will soon be enriched with new ARCEP measures and with collectivities' and partners' data.

The website "Cartefibre.arcep.fr" presents fiber coverage information on usual administrative levels and on individual buildings, and so to track the progress of Fiber to the home rollouts in a detailed fashion.

"Ma connexion internet", in a beta version, presents a map-based search engine for monitoring national fixed network coverage for all technologies combined, at the individual address level.

Regarding *"J'alerte l'ARCEP"*

The platform allows any user, whether an individual, a business or a local authority, to report a malfunction they have encountered in their relationship with their fixed or mobile telephone operator, internet service provider or postal operator. The platform has two objectives:

For the users: to create an opportunity for them to influence market regulation, to encourage operators to improve their services and further develop their networks. It also allows users to rapidly obtain advice tailored to their circumstances.

For ARCEP: to enable it to track the problems encountered by users in real time. The ability to draw on recurrent malfunctions, and detect both spikes in user alerts and weak signals to target its actions, and to be more effective in its regulatory actions.

Results, impact and lessons learnt

The results of the publication of maps can be measured quantitatively. For example the website "*monreseaumobile*" was visited by 740 000 visitors and the website "*cartefibre*" by 555 000 visitors for the year 2018. More importantly, the publication of such information generated a lot of feedbacks and suggestions for improvement. This appropriation of the tools by collectivities, users, associations but also actors from the telecom sector (like small operators) demonstrated the usefulness of the tools and the need for these tools to be updated and enriched regularly.

The open data associated to these publications have been a very interesting element. By making data openly available ARCEP wanted to allow third parties to access and use them, talk about them, bring new value to them and produce relevant tools for user. This worked to a certain extend as some actors came to reuse our data for purposes that we did not identify at the beginning: to evaluate the coverage quality of transports or schools for example but also to help hikers or customers. But this approach also revealed that analysing data is not easy for general users and that if public actors want to make open data real they have not only to make data available but to develop a real strategy of publication (format, structure, interface, etc.) adapted to the different users.

ARCEP received about 90 000 alerts in three years: close to five times more than in the years preceding the launch of "*J'alerte l'ARCEP*", including 71 000 posted directly via the platform.

These alerts enabled ARCEP to examine several concrete cases and identify specific issues or systemic problems that may not have been identified otherwise, or too late. To be more concrete, some specific issues can be identified instantaneously when they come up and be analysed very quickly by ARCEP's staff giving the opportunity to fix the problem with the concerned operators., Other issues are more complex and need more time to be fully identified., The resolution process is then longer and involves a thorough study with operators.

Depending on the problems encountered, ARCEP could adapt its answer: from calling the concerned operators involved in real time in order to find a rapid solution, to opening an official investigation (based on the provisions of CPCE Article L. 36-11). A report[1] providing the first scorecard of the "*J'alerte l'ARCEP*" user reporting platform after one year of operation has been published including some analysis and examples of action generated.

Co-operation

In France, in July 2019 eight French independent authorities (*Autorité des Marchés Financiers, Autorité de Régulation des Transports*, ARCEP, *Autorité de Régulation des Jeux En Ligne, Autorité de la Concurrence, Commission Nationale de l'Informatique et des Libertés, Commission Régulation de l'Énergie* and *Conseil Supérieur de l'Audiovisuel*) adopted a common note[2] on data-driven regulation. As data-driven regulation creates the ability to make stakeholders more accountable, increases the regulator's capacity for analysis and makes more information available to users and civil society, we collectively acknowledged that these goals are not sectorial specific. Therefore, in this dedicated memorandum the seven regulators share their common views and good practices on the use of data with other authorities and deliver an account of the progress made on data-driven regulation.

At international level, the document on mobile coverage and quality of service published at the 2019 network of French-speaking telecommunications regulators (Fratel) annual meeting worth to be mentioned. The purpose of this document is to deliver an outline of current data collection, use and publication practices. It sets out for authorities the key focal points for ensuring that mobile quality of service and coverage data are published under the best possible conditions and includes reference to some of the initiatives adopted by ARCEP as part of its data driven approach. These works will continue in 2020. In line with the theme of coverage and quality of service, the network will start work on the feasibility of an online tool on the representation of coverage and quality of mobile service in the member countries of the network.

ARCEP's views on digital platforms regulation

ARCEP deems that a supervision of platforms allowed by *ex ante* regulation, which allows rapid intervention when necessary, before the damage materialises, would have significant advantages. This supervision should be based on a graduated approach which would propose a typology of remedies appropriate to the damage observed: monitoring of platforms, transparency of certain essential algorithms used by platforms, portability of essential data, interoperability.

In this regard, such a "data-driven regulation" could be one of the key tools to regulate digital platforms. First, it gives the power directly back to the people (not to the State): consumers, entrepreneurs, NGOs, academics. It is thus well suited for the digital ecosystem where decentralisation is more prominent. Secondly, providing more transparency might be a really efficient quick win as digital platforms are especially opaque.

Notes

[1] ARCEP Press Release, Data-Driven Regulation, 2019, https://en.arcep.fr/news/press-releases/view/n/data-driven-regulation-4.html.

[2] ARCEP Press Release, Cooperation between Regulators, https://en.arcep.fr/news/press-releases/p/n/cooperation-between-regulators.html.

Impacts of digital transformation on markets and regulation in the French land transport sector: Case study on the Transport Regulatory Authority (ART)

Context

Passenger transport in Europe is undergoing a profound transformation, due in no small part to the digitalisation of mobility.

Digital transformation in the transport sector has numerous advantages for consumers, as it translates in particular into:

- new uses of existing modes (e.g. car sharing)
- new entrants and increased supply of services (e.g. Uber cabs)
- new tools to compare transport modes and prices and improve multimodality (comparators, route planners, interoperable ticketing systems, etc.)
- increased capacities to characterise and target demand (big data)
- competitive pressures on monopolies (e.g. rail) as intermodal competition is facilitated.

On the supply side, new frontiers are emerging in competition between transport modes so that competition becomes more and more intermodal. On top of what new business models and new transport policies are being developed.

Issues

In that context, the French Transport Regulatory Authority (*Autorité de régulation des transports*, ART) has identified some new challenges posed to regulators:

First, increased competition between transport modes due to digitalisation questions the definition of relevant markets and, in turn, the definition of dominant positions. Some of the underlying questions include: should regulators (transport regulatory bodies as well as competition authorities) maintain a modal approach or define relevant markets as multimodal? How and to what extent should regulators take into account the risks associated with transport operators' diversification (leverage effect)?

In addition, increased competition between transport modes also inevitably questions the scope of intervention of transport regulators and their capacities to analyse and take into account intermodal competition (e.g. between trains and coaches or between air-planes and high-speed trains) to efficiently regulate. Some of the underlying questions include: Is it relevant to maintain "mono-modal" regulators? Shouldn't transport regulators be multimodal transport regulators?

Finally, with digitalisation, the control of intangible assets like data by transport operators may increase the risks of exclusionary conducts. As observed when the airline transport market was liberalised, the control over computerised reservation systems by incumbent transport companies may be used to foreclose competitors on the downstream markets. Similarly, the control over information/data on traffic, timetables, customer bases, etc. may provide a non-replicable advantage causing the exclusion of competitors on the transport market. Some of the underlying questions include: To what extent should transport regulators (and more generally sectoral regulators) be in charge of guaranteeing fair, transparent and non-discriminatory access to intangible assets/facilities that affects the intensity of competition on the transport service market?

Approach and intervention

If digitalisation is a challenge for regulators, it is also an opportunity. Indeed, digital technologies are potentially opening many avenues to reduce information asymmetries between operators, users and regulators and, in the end, allow the latter to better perform their tasks.

New technologies mean increased capacities for regulators to collect, stock and process existing data on the upstream and downstream markets and open the black box of monopolies. It further allows a better control of the performance of regulated companies and, ultimately, it is a source of incentives as it reduces information asymmetries and allows to better challenging regulated firms' efficiency.

The new powers given to ART in 2015 and the on-going transposition of the Regulation No. 2017/1926 on the provision of EU-wide multimodal travel information services are two recent measures that ART would like to highlight for the purpose of this case study.

Toward a data-driven regulation

In 2015, the French Transport Regulatory Authority (ART) was legally empowered to collect data from land transport companies and sanction non-co-operative behaviours. Since then, it has implemented a data-driven regulation. Actions taken include:

- creation of a market monitoring department (with statisticians, economists, data scientists)
- data collection campaigns on a regular basis (NB: several appeals were lodged against our data requests, all rejected by the Court)
- field surveys
- systematic reporting and publication of results and benchmarking (yardstick + sunshine regulation)
- organisation of a hackathon (19 March 2019) to develop an "app" improving the information disclosed to users on rail service quality.

From databased transport regulation to the regulation of transport data

To encourage the development of new services facilitating multimodal journeys (transport route planner together or not with through ticketing, real-time arbitrage solutions), the EU Commission adopted Regulation No. 2017/1926 on 31 May 2017. Regulation No. 2017/1926 defines, for each mode of transport (regular/on demand; public/private; urban/interurban), the perimeter and format of the data on transport that various stakeholders (private operators, public operators, organising authorities) will have to make available according to a precise agenda. It further requires stakeholders to provide static data related to theoretical transport offer (schedule, stops, fares, journey time) as well as dynamic data on real-time traffic disturbances for instance.

An act transposing Regulation No. 2017/1926 (*Loi d'orientation des mobilités*) was adopted in France in December 2019. Among other things, it stipulates that:

- All local authorities will have to organise mobility and will be responsible for the provision of multimodal information system.

- ART will be in charge of controlling the proper implementation of data opening (includes the power to settle disputes and fine data providers in case of non-compliance to their obligations), and the absence of bias of the information on travel options provided to customers.

Results, impact and lessons learnt

The main lesson learnt based on ART's experience is that databased regulatory decisions certainly increase the credibility of regulators and objectify public debates.

Concrete examples of ART's recent actions include:

- update of crucial regulatory hypotheses (e.g. induction rate, occupancy rate, pricing unit of access charges, price elasticity of demand…);
- revision of rail transport service quality indicators (punctuality and reliability);
- forthcoming tool (app) based on machine learning to calculate the likelihood of traffic disturbance on the rail network at a very disaggregated level.

For a data-driven regulation to be effective and credible, it is a pre-requisite for the regulator to have the legal powers to collect data and to sanction the non-compliance to data transmission obligations. Indeed, regulated companies may be reluctant to disclose information on their action and performance, as illustrated by the appeals against ART's requests for data from railway undertakings. Finally having sufficient financial and human resources will be decisive for the regulator to become a data cruncher and make the most of the opportunity offered by digitalisation.

Co-operation

To develop a common approach to data-driven regulation, seven French regulators (Competition Authority (ADLC), Financial Market Authority (AMF), Telecommunications Regulatory Body (ARCEP), Data Protection Authority (CNIL), Energy Regulatory Body (CRE), Broadcasting Authority (CSA) and Transport Regulatory Authority (ART)) issued in July 2019 a dedicated memorandum which formalises their thought processes and delivers an account of the progress they have made in this area.

The "Energy and Mobility" Datathon jointly organised by ART and CRE in March 2019 is one particular example of co-operation between national regulatory authorities aiming at pooling human and financial resources to develop innovative regulatory tools (web/mobile apps). The challenges proposed to participants indeed included the creation of BtoC tools which reuse the two regulators' own data in a relevant way, to foster interactivity with end users and allow them, first, to obtain information that is not currently shared by operators (or not sufficiently accurate) and, second, to send information to the regulators (e.g. on malfunctions).

Enhancing foresight capacity to enlighten the future of the energy sector and its regulation in France: Case study on the Energy Regulatory Commission (CRE)

Context

The French energy regulator, i.e. *Commission de régulation de l'énergie* (CRE) was established on 24 March 2000 by the French law on the modernisation and development of the public electricity service of 10 February 2000. The creation of CRE is part of the impetus for the energy market liberalisation following the first electricity and gas European directives, respectively in 1996 and 1998. However, the law of 10 February 2000 exceeds the initial requirements of the directives, which did not impose the creation of a regulatory authority. This will require waiting for Directive 2003/54 of 26 June 2003.

CRE aims at contributing to the smooth functioning of the electricity and natural gas markets for the benefit of consumers, and at ensuring that there is no discrimination, cross-subsidisation or interference with competition. Composed of a board of five members appointed based on their legal, economic and technical qualifications for a non-renewable six-year term, CRE is currently chaired by Jean-François Carenco, appointed by presidential decree of 16 February 2017.

Legally speaking, CRE is an independent administrative authority. According to the French Senate report for the evaluation of legislation on 15 June 2006, it is "the adaptability of independent administrative authorities to their missions, which makes each of them an original entity, and constitutes one of their main assets".

As a consequence of its legal DNA, CRE has continually evolved and sought to anticipate future challenges in the energy sector, in order to adapt the regulatory framework and to foster energy markets. This need to adapt has never been so important at a time of structural changes in the energy sector and participate to the so-called "dynamic regulation".

Issues

Indeed, energy stakeholders face today two major developments: the energy transition and the digital revolution. Regarding the energy transition, it shall be recalled that the Paris agreement of December 2015, the energy transition law for green growth of 2015 and the European Package for clean energy of 2016 outline collective actions to be carried out, regarding industrial, social and economic challenges. The need to reduce CO_2 emissions leads to limiting the share of fossil fuels in the energy mix while the consequences of Fukushima require, in public opinion, to diversify energy sources. A major industrial development is underway. On one hand, renewable energies succeed in lowering their production costs, on the other hand, grids need to be adapted, upstream to the increased intermittence of generation and, downstream the downward trend in energy demand. The energy world therefore has all the tools it needs to design an industry and consumption that respects a preserved planet. Subject to an energy policy of great control, generating and consuming non-polluting energies is possible in the medium term and on a large scale without declining prosperity, the quality of supply or jeopardizing collective progress.

At the same time, the pace and scale of digital integration in society do not only create new tools but also transform productive and consumption capacities. The entire energy chain will be affected: from a more affordable renewable generation, supported by innovative storage technologies, to the new power of consumers who can have consumption (and production) control means.

These major developments create a particularly uncertain future and challenge the functioning of the energy markets.

Approach and intervention

For the above mentioned reasons, the President of CRE, Jean François Carenco decided to create an area dedicated to reflection, exchange and information sharing, namely the *Comité de prospective* (foresight committee).

Created on 17 October 2017, this committee is an innovative approach for the market, as well as for CRE, to assess how regulators can face future challenges. By doing so, it supports CRE to anticipate, identify and understand forward-looking main issues in the energy sector at medium and long-term (2030 and 2050). The foresight committee has two objectives: i) to provide expertise to CRE and energy stakeholders; ii) to implement successful energy transition and to put the digital revolution at the service of all electricity and gas consumer, in a multidisciplinary and collective prospective action.

It gathers all energy stakeholders from:

- generation (EDF, Engie, Total, etc.);
- transportation and distributions operators (RTE, Enedis, GRT gaz, Téréga, GRDF, etc.);
- private (Schneider electric, Gimélec, Atos, etc.), alternative (Anode,FIEG) and environmental entities (ADEME);
- representatives of the energy sector (AFG, UFE,etc.);
- renewable energies companies or unions (SER);
- mobility sector (Avere France); consumers association (AFL); a think tank dedicated to urban innovation (La Fabrique de la Cité);
- consulting firm specialised in energy (NégaWatt);
- academics (Tours, Paris-Dauphine Universities); French energy ombudsman (MNE);
- elected local officials and members of the Parliament.

To prepare its prospective approach, CRE commissioned a first external preparatory study elaborated by the E-Cube Strategy Consultants, with nine monographs. This general study, published[1] on 30 May 2018, enriched the work of the foresight committee and reported on major global reflections on structural energy issues. Twelve issues (Table 2.1) were then chosen to propose national (and perhaps European) level regulatory approaches, to adapt to a rapidly changing sector. They describe a largely remodelled energy sector, under the combined effects of technological evolutions and public politics in response to social stakes. They were submitted to a board of 80 international energy experts, not related to the foresight committee. The results of this study[2] were presented at European level during the General Assembly of the Council of European Energy Regulators in September 2018.

Chaired by the President of CRE, the 46-member steering committee of the foresight committee includes business and academic leaders and representatives of institutions and associations in the energy sector. Each year since 2018, the steering group launches new research on three different topics, divided into three working groups articulated around the energy chain logic: upstream issues (energy mix), grids one (flexibility, storage) and downstream issues (consumer). Due to its success, a fourth working group was created in 2020, with a focus on integrated vision, from upstream to downstream of the energy chain.[3]

Table 2.1. Twelve reflection paths for the regulator

1	In France as in Europe, adjusting regulatory approaches to account for a faster deployment pace of innovative technologies (storage, flexibility, metering, data), and their impacts on operators.
2	Generalising frames experiments to answer the complexity of emerging market design issues, through approaches such as the "regulatory sandboxes".
3	Developing a regulatory framework to improve coordination between new generation capacities deployment and grids development.
4	Exercising caution in new natural gas system investments (except those related to security of supply or green gas development), to avoid stranded costs if low gas demand scenarios were to realise.
5	Improving the quality of economic signals conveyed to economic actors, to avoid long-term and costly repercussions of faulty mechanisms.
6	Applying these principles to self-consumption.
7	Ensuring that the market configuration produces relevant long-term economic signals for investments.
8	Facilitating the emergence of incentive mechanisms other than subsidies, relying as much as possible on market-based mechanisms, to encourage renewable energy development.
9	Setting-up a governance allowing for the coordination between TSO and DSO operations when mobilising distributed flexibility resources.
10	Improving the coordination between operators and actors of the electric and gas systems, to facilitate an overall approach to the development and operation of the energy system.
11	Allowing for distributed storage development.
12	Ensuring consumer trust in the context of a rapidly evolving sector.

In parallel, the committee also carries out international observation and study missions in places representative of an ambitious investment in the energies of the future. Thus, the first season of the foresight committee led its members in two countries: i) the first study visit took place in California around the Silicon Valley, which has set ambitious goals: 40% of CO_2 emission reduction in 2030 compared to 1990, to reach 50% renewable energy and 5 million electric vehicles – with major issues management of its new forms of energy in the grid and an important need for storage; ii) members of the committee then went to China, world's leading producer of original electricity photovoltaic and wind power with a strong state will to massively develop electric cars and to lower the cost of batteries. The second season field trips took place in French territories, as the main topic focused on decentralisation.[4]

Results, impact and lessons learnt

On 5 July 2018, the CRE foresight committee presented its first three reports. Based on monthly working groups, which gathered over 200 experts, these reports aimed at favouring the emergence of several long-term consensus, and to suggest solutions to support the transformations of the sector.

After two seasons, the foresight committee has successfully fulfilled its missions. As it is intended, it definitely appears as a multidisciplinary area for exchanges and analyses for energy experts. The work of the foresight committee also expands CRE horizons in two ways. On one hand, international and European benchmarking studies are fully integrated in the foresight committee works. In addition, various field and study trips in France, within the European Union and abroad, offer different ways of thinking and possibilities to achieve market mechanisms.

As the energy regulator is the place of independence, neutrality, public service, equality and the general interest, the foresight committee is actually the unique forum in France for various energy stakeholders where they can freely debate with a high level of expertise on medium and long-term trends.

Such area gives opportunities to build relations, to anticipate possible conflicts and to identify major future stakes. Furthermore, the publication of this abundant work is a major and unique source of information, open to all, on innovations and their consequences, which can enlighten decision-makers in their own field skill.

The work done was highly appreciated by all the members of the foresight committee, which now appears as the front door of the regulatory strategy and innovation. Thus, the collective reflection and the very wide and diverse panel of actors are also of great interest for CRE teams. Indeed, two mains reports of the foresight committee have brought attention: the impact of green mobility on the energy mix, notably the part on electric vehicles, and the storage one. Those two reports had significant impact on visions and works of the committee, but also of CRE services. This led CRE to be aware of two large scales topics and to publish two dedicated reports from a more regulatory and technical perspectives.

It is why CRE launched in October 2018 a broad reflection on the electrical networks serving electric vehicles. For several months, the services met with around fifty actors, organised a forum, three workshops and interviewed their European counterparts. Based on all these exchanges, CRE published the first conclusions and lines of study arising from this project in order to inform the public debate, in particular the discussions around the mobility orientation bill.

CRE also undertook work on storage issue and published in September 2019 its roadmap to set up a legal, technical and economic framework enabling sustainable storage development, in line with the French energy system and the national energy policy. Following the call for contributions launched in the first quarter of 2019, CRE defined a work program, addressed requests to grid operators and formulated recommendations to public authorities for actions within their competencies. Since then, grid operators have clarified and adapted some of the market rules to enable the participation of storage (in particular the FCR and the RR) and simplified the connection rules for storage. Some of the actions defined in the work program will be done at a later time: connection rules will gradually take into account characteristics of storage and the market - rules will be adapted, for instance, to enable the participation of hybrid sites (renewable generation and storage). At the same time, CRE organises workshops with stakeholders to communicate on the progress of the roadmap.

The works of the foresight committee are not predictive but they help regulator to be fully aware of the scale and quick changes, and to adapt his regulatory methods in order to not only encourage innovation among market players, but also innovate on his working methods.

A dedicated website *Eclairer l'avenir* ("enlight the future") is available at: http://www.eclairerlavenir.fr/ (only in French for the moment).

Notes

[1] CRE, 2018, Étude sur les perspectives stratégiques dans le secteur de l'énergie [Study on strategic perspectives in the energy sector], http://www.eclairerlavenir.fr/etude-sur-les-perspectives-strategiques-dans-le-secteur-de-lenergie/ .

[2] CRE, 2018, Presentation of the Sounding Board Results – Study on strategic perspectives on energy, http://fichiers.cre.fr/Etude-perspectives-strategiques/4PanelExperts/Sounding_Board_Results_EN.pdf.

[3] Programme for 2020 can be accessed at the following link: http://www.eclairerlavenir.fr/edition-2020-du-comite-de-prospective-plaquette-de-presentation/

The working themes for the 2020 season are :

- **WG1** Bouquet énergétique, "Marine energies" co-chaired by Marc LAFOSSE, President of Énergie de la Lune and President of the Marine Energies Commission of SER and Jérôme PECRESSE, President and CEO of GE Renewable Energy who delegated his co-chairmanship to Hugh BAILEY, CEO of General Electric France;
- **WG2** Energy Networks and Systems, "New Cities, New Networks" co-chaired by Claude ARNAUD, President of the Efficacity Research & Development Institute and Bernard BOUCAULT, Honorary Prefect of the Region;
- **WG3** Consumer and Society, "Downstream metering" co-chaired by Cécile MAISONNEUVE, President of the Fabrique de la Cité and Fabien CHONÉ, co-founder of Direct Energie and President of Fabelsi ;
- **WG4** Integrated Vision, "The Hydrogen Vector" co-chaired by Olivier APPERT, member of the Académie des Technologies and Patrice GEOFFRON, Professor of Economics at the University of Paris-Dauphine and Director of the Centre for Geopolitics of Energy and Raw Materials (CGEMP).

[4] Twenty-two trips are envisaged for all the WGs either in the "small committee" format, governance of the Foresight Committee and co-chairs, or in the "extended group" format for all the members of the working group. These visits accompany the Season 3 guideline: industry (The second guideline of Season 3: socio-technical issues, is approached via bilateral talks between the Foresight Committee and social science researchers).

These visits concern industrial and demonstrator sites as well as meetings with local elected officials in charge of energy skills or project management to hear their needs and expectations concerning the evolution of the legislative and regulatory framework that would facilitate the conduct of their innovative development projects.

Most of the trips concern France: Nice metropolis, Jupiter 1 000 demonstrators, Dunkerque wind power plant, offshore wind farm in Brittany, Marne-la-Vallée eco-neighbourhood, etc. And one in Germany is under discussion.

How EPA Ireland is using new technologies in its regulatory processes: Case study on the Environmental Protection Agency (EPA)

Institution and relevant market / context information

The Environmental Protection Agency (EPA) is at the front line of environmental protection and policing in Ireland. The EPA is an independent public body established under the Environmental Protection Agency Act, 1992. The EPA has a wide range of knowledge, regulatory and advocacy functions including responsibility for environmental licensing and enforcement of industrial, waste and wastewater activities.

Data management technologies and practices have undergone dramatic transformation since 1992. In 1992, our regulatory information and all interactions between the EPA and its licensees were recorded in paper files, which gradually evolved into electronic document storage. From 2005 to 2015, the EPA invested significant ICT time and effort in developing database management systems (DBMS). Important features of the EPA data management architecture are the Environmental Data Exchange Network (EDEN), a Microsoft CRM application to manage all authorisations data and a centralised database of environmental geographic (GIS) data. For more information please see Annex Figure 2.A.1.

In 2017, the EPA adopted an enterprise architecture approach to ICT portfolio management and examined the ICT organisational structure. The EPA had achieved a great deal in establishing robust data management systems: the next opportunity was to unlock the potential of this structured data to gather more knowledge and insights about Ireland's environment. In 2018, the EPA established a small Analytics team of four staff and two contractors to pilot the use of data science, spatial analysis, earth observation and data visualisation techniques. The purpose of the team is to analyse data to generate knowledge and insights on the environment by working collaboratively with EPA subject matter experts. When the team of experts was formed they embarked on a series of stakeholder meetings across the EPA to identify opportunities for the application of data science and analysis. The idea for this project came from a stakeholder meeting. The project was prioritised because:

- the data was available to make it a feasible project to deliver quickly, and,
- the importance of UWW treatment to the protection of human health and water quality indicated that it would be a project that would have high environmental impact.

Problem

The EPA regulates more than 1 000 urban waste water treatment plants (small to large). The plants are operated by Ireland's water utility company Irish Water. A small team of eleven EPA inspectors check that these plants are operating safely within their emission limit values (ELV) and meeting all the conditions of their environmental licenses. All the administrative data about the plants is stored in a Microsoft CRM database. Monitoring results from the environment upstream and downstream of the plants are stored in a Laboratory Information System: seven different parameters are monitored. The EPA has access to thousands of data points about Ireland's waste water treatment plants. This is a rich resource but the data needed to be organised and presented in a way that allows the team of eleven EPA inspectors to quickly identify issues at the plants without repeatedly examining hundreds and thousands of data points.

Approach and intervention

In its simplest terms the job of a waste water treatment plant is to take in dirty water and remove pollutants from it before discharging that water back into the environment. The effectiveness of a plant can be measured by comparing the quality of water entering the plant (the influent) to the quality of the water leaving (the effluent). If a plant is operating effectively then the effluent water should be clean: the monitoring results for any of the seven parameters should return results that are below the Emission Limit Value. Irish Water monitor the influent and effluent water and submit their results to the EPA via the web based Environmental Data Exchange Network (EDEN) portal.

The Analytics team identified an opportunity to assess the UWWT data and use statistical methods (integrating multiple results over a number of cycles to produce period trends) to group the monitoring results into "improving", "staying the same" or "getting worse" for each of the different parameters to produce an Urban Waste Water Scorecard. This would allow an Inspector to examine all their plants and quickly focus on the specific plants and parameters that were a problem or "trending" towards failure.

The data analysts isolated the monitoring data for each parameter at each emission point for each waste water treatment plant. Then the data is manipulated to assess how efficient the plant is at removing each parameter. The available influent and effluent data are aggregated as monthly averages. A monthly efficiency value is determined by expressing the monthly effluent figure as a percentage of the monthly influent figure. A metric is applied to the set of monthly efficiency values that measures if the plant performance is either improving or deteriorating for this parameter over the last three years.

Then the rate of ELV compliance for each parameter is analysed. A calculation is applied to express the annual rate of compliance based on the number of effluent results that breach the ELV threshold each year. A metric is applied to the annual compliance rates of the past three years to express whether the plant performance is getting better or worse for each parameter over the previous three years.

The outcome is a prototype dashboard that summarises the trends at each wastewater treatment plant using clear graphics (see Figure 2.3).

Figure 2.3. Urban Waste Water Scorecard graphics

P.E. Load	ELV Compliant	Ammonia	BOD
78.55	✔	—	—
71.18	✔	—	—
85.99	✘	—	↑

Notes: The load on the plant (P.E. or population equivalent) is colour coded as green for within limits, amber for close to load and red for overloaded. A green tick means the plant meets its Emission Limit Values overall, a red X means it does not. A green arrow under a parameter means the effluent results for this parameter are improving, a grey hyphen means the results are staying the same and a red arrow means the effluent results for this parameter are getting worse).
Source: information provided by EPA, 2019.

The Inspector can click through on a plant to see graphs of the monitoring results for any of the seven parameters. There are three graphs: influent results, effluent results and the monthly removal coefficient (see Figure 2.4).

Figure 2.4. Sample compliance monitoring results graph

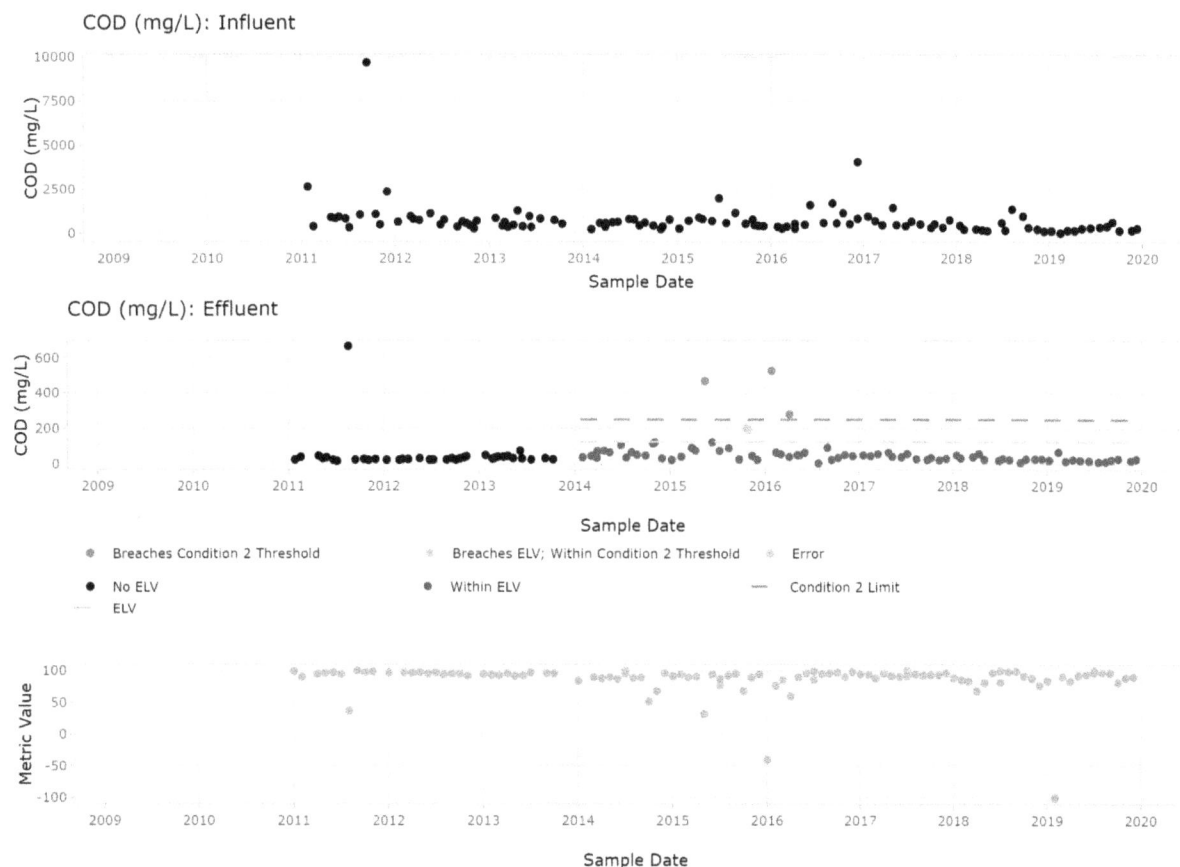

Source: information provided by EPA. 2019.

The Inspector can see the trend for each parameter. If a plant's performance is declining, then the monitoring results for the effluent will start to drift towards an ELV limit line: interventions should be taken well before an ELV is breached. The monthly removal co-efficient will also start to trend downwards: the removal coefficient has a seasonal trend but over time the whole profile starts to trend downwards if a plant's performance is declining. Presenting the data in this way makes it easy for an inspector to see if a change in plant performance is an anomaly or indicative of a systemic failure at the plant.

The graphs can also be used to confirm effectiveness of interventions and improvements. The graph below shows the dramatic improvement in the effluent monitoring after an upgrade to a treatment plant in the south east of Ireland (see Figure 2.5). There is an opportunity to expand the methods to allow an Inspector to model the impact of new connections to the sewage network that would increase the load on plant, or to model the expected impacts of new investments to improve the plant.

Figure 2.5. Sample compliance monitoring results showing impact of plant upgrade from 2014 onwards

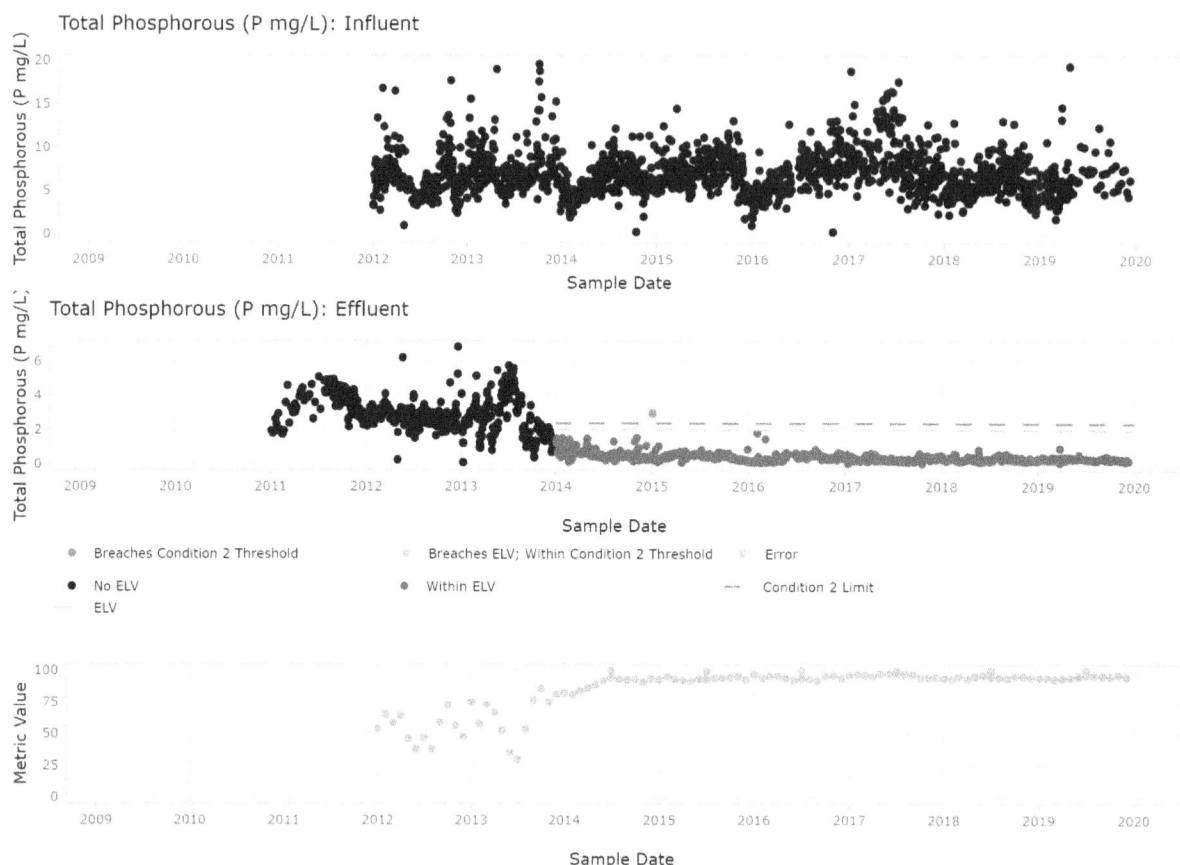

Source: information provided by EPA. 2019.

Results, impact and lessons learnt

The result of the prototype was proof of the concept that the application of statistical techniques to monitoring data leads to more insights into the patterns and trends of monitoring results. The overall "performance indicator" derived from assessment of many factors is innovative and unique. The time input required from the Analytics team was six weeks of one data analyst to analyse the problem, develop the scripts and create the prototype dashboard.

This would not be straightforward without a structured database of frequent monitoring results (i.e. the one version of the truth). The lesson learned is that investment in database management systems and good data management processes can be capitalised on quite easily with a small investment of time from a data analyst. If the data was not structured and well managed to start with then the prototype would have taken a lot more effort and would be difficult to maintain.

The impacts of the urban waste water scorecard are:

- Inspectors can more readily adopt a risk based enforcement approach using the "getting worse" flags in the scorecard. Efficiencies can be achieved by presenting the data to Inspectors so that they can quickly zone in on problem sites.
- Inspectors can verify that the works on the plant have contributed to improving downstream water quality; this evidence is useful in creating river basin management plans.

- A large volume of data from different sources was made accessible to UWWT Inspectors. This had two benefits. The first was extra insights: the calculation of metrics provided the inspectors with insights into what a large volume of monitoring data was telling them about the UWWT plant performance. The second was accessibility – presenting the data in a single dashboard interface made it easy for the Inspectors to access. Traditionally this would be reported as a saving in staff time, communicated as FTE. Time is indeed saved but this is only one aspect of a range of benefits that are harder to quantify in traditional measures like FTE. Accessibility of data, with additional insights, makes it easier to make decisions, communicate decisions and have confidence in the decisions. Anecdotally the Inspectors report that having this kind of access to data – and metrics – makes it easier for them to assess the situation at a UWWT plant and to be confident in their interactions with the UWWT operators.

Analytics is an emerging area in the EPA: the prototype dashboard is a good way to showcase the potential of analytics techniques. As a working example of analytics techniques in action it allows other EPA teams to understand the potential of analytics and how it could benefit their own work areas. The creation of this expert team allowed for an analytical use of UWWT data. UWWT inspectors would have been able to collate and analyse the data but did not have the time to do so, or the technical skills in R programming to create the reproducible metrics and dashboard. Setting up a team of experts with data analysis and technical skills means the EPA has the capacity to build metrics and tools that teams can apply to their day to day work.

Other examples of how other EPA teams use similar analytics techniques to enhance their regulatory decisions and outcomes

The team of experts is working with other EPA teams and is applying data analysis in different ways to the UWWT case study that was submitted. In brief:

- The team of experts worked with the EPA Laboratory teams on a prototype dashboard that is similar to the UWWT example. The laboratory teams collect monitoring data from our authorised facilities. The prototype demonstrated more dynamic ways for the lab teams to share their data with the EPA enforcement teams.

- The team of experts is working with the Greenhouse Gas emissions inventory and projections team on a feasibility study to see if EPA can use a land-use map as the data source for annual Land Use, Land Use Change & Forestry (LULUCF) regulation reporting. This is using spatial analysis and remote sensing techniques.

- The team of experts is working with the EPA radon team to assess the feasibility of updating the national radon risk map (a radon risk map is referenced in Ireland's building regulations). The team of experts is using data verification and spatial analysis techniques here rather than prototyping.

- The team of experts is at the early stages of developing a project with the EPA waste enforcement team to examine the potential of analytics for waste data analysis.

The process of raising awareness of the potential of analytics across the EPA is an ongoing one. It is made easier by having a bank of prototypes and completed projects as this gives EPA teams something to relate to so that they can imagine their own uses for analytics techniques. For more information please see Annex 2.B.

Annex 2.A. EPA Ireland data journey

Annex Figure 2.A.1. EPA Ireland data journey

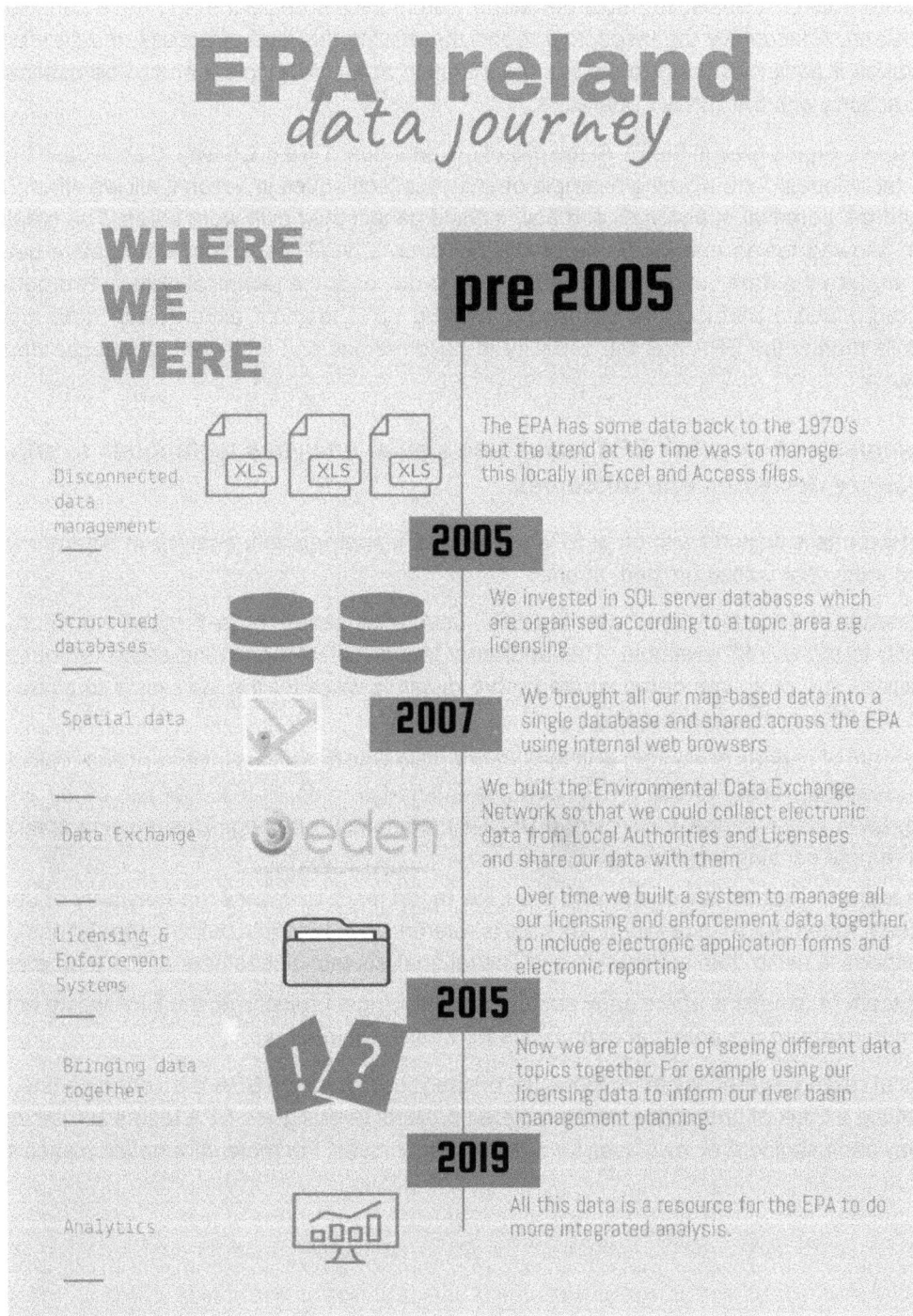

Source: information provided by EPA. 2019.

Annex 2.B. EPA Analytics team

How was the need to establish this team identified? What was the process to approve and fund its creation and to set it up (i.e. recruitment, finding appropriate capacity, internal resistance)?

The seeds were sown for this activity many years ago with the establishment of a small environmental informatics unit. This unit developed the first EPA website circa 1997. In the late nineties and early noughties the EPA began to expand its GIS and spatial analysis capability mainly through research fellows linked to Universities but based in the EPA. Some of these, in time, became staff of the EPA. Over time, the informatics team became more involved in the development and project management of IT products with less time available for assessment work.

The 2016-2020 EPA Strategy established a goal for the EPA to be organisationally excellent. One planned outcome was enhanced capacity in the area of organisational change and in the use of ICT to support reform and innovation.

In 2017 the EPA established a temporary Enterprise Architecture project team to reorganise and re-align the EPA ICT resources through the implementation of integrated structures. For this review the team:

- Had site visits with peer organisations in the public and private sector to learn from their approaches.
- Created a business capability model and a technology capability model that mapped out the capabilities the EPA needed to successfully run its day to day business.
- Assessed the maturity of these two models to identify the current state of the EPA's capabilities versus where it needed to be to achieve its 2016-2020 strategy.
- Reviewed the ICT structures with input from EPA ICT staff.

This review process identified that the EPA had invested significantly in building up robust database management systems. There was opportunity to make more use of the data. Setting up a small team with the purpose of analysing data to gain knowledge and insights would allow the EPA to take this opportunity.

The Enterprise Architecture project team proposed a new ICT structure to the EPA Board of Directors. The new structure included a proposal to move three staff and two contractors with data analysis, spatial analysis and remote sensing skills to a new Analytics team. This proposal was approved by the EPA Board in June 2017. The team was placed in the EPA Evidence program and given a small budget from EPA core funds. No recruitment was necessary as existing staff were redeployed. The staff had been doing ICT development and maintenance work so backfilling the staff was a challenge: 12 months elapsed before all the staff could be completely assigned to analytics work. The team reported to the EPA Board of Directors in July 2018 to update them on the progress of the team (copy of memo attached) in defining a rolling workplan, establishing the skills the team needed to develop, inter and intra agency communications required and standards that needed to be defined for the practice of analytics in the EPA.

Based on this successful project, what are the other areas that the team will be working on? What are some of the overall results and impact on the work of the EPA that you expect from the team and its work?

The EPA produced a State of the Environment Report in 2016 (Ireland's Environment: An Assessment 2016). This report identified seven key actions (Annex Figure 2.B.1). These key actions can also be mapped to the UN Sustainable Development Goals.

Annex Figure 2.B.1. The seven key actions from Ireland's Environment: An Assessment 2016

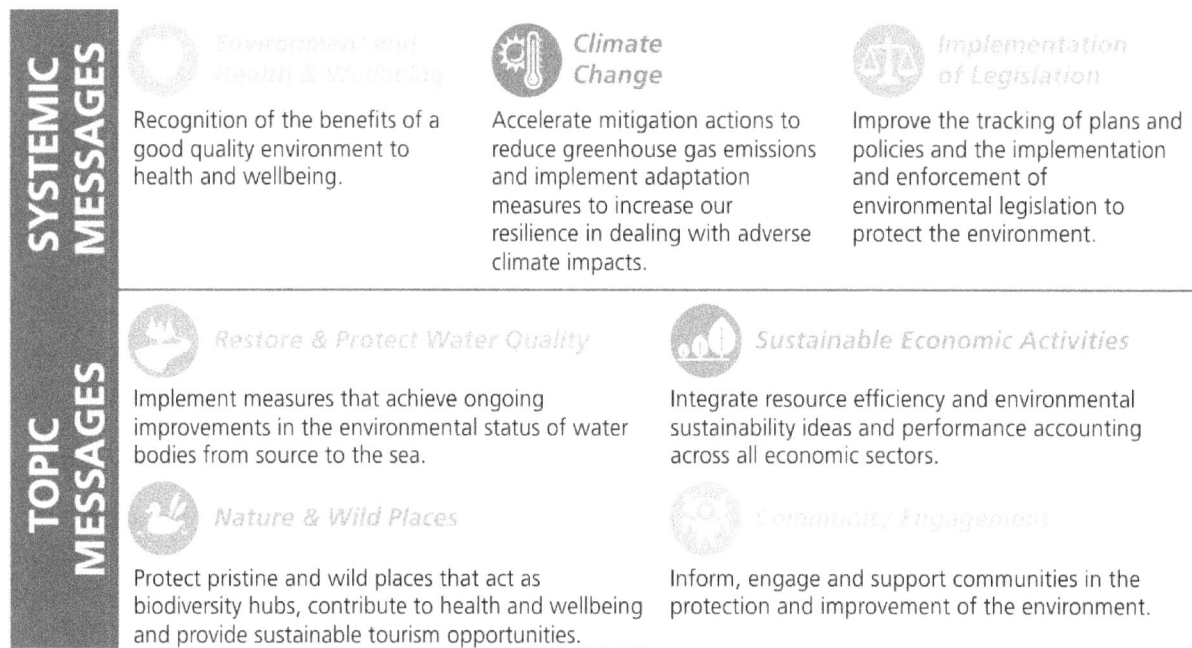

SYSTEMIC MESSAGES	Environment and Health & Wellbeing	Climate Change	Implementation of Legislation
	Recognition of the benefits of a good quality environment to health and wellbeing.	Accelerate mitigation actions to reduce greenhouse gas emissions and implement adaptation measures to increase our resilience in dealing with adverse climate impacts.	Improve the tracking of plans and policies and the implementation and enforcement of environmental legislation to protect the environment.

TOPIC MESSAGES	Restore & Protect Water Quality	Sustainable Economic Activities
	Implement measures that achieve ongoing improvements in the environmental status of water bodies from source to the sea.	Integrate resource efficiency and environmental sustainability ideas and performance accounting across all economic sectors.
	Nature & Wild Places	Community Engagement
	Protect pristine and wild places that act as biodiversity hubs, contribute to health and wellbeing and provide sustainable tourism opportunities.	Inform, engage and support communities in the protection and improvement of the environment.

Source: information provided by EPA, 2019.

The Analytics team categorise their work plan around these seven key actions. The team reviewed the State of the Environment Report, held 30 internal stakeholder meetings and created a list of project ideas (with expected outcomes) for projects in each of the seven key action areas. The ideas are initiated as projects based on perceived value (urgency and expected impact of the issue or question), feasibility (available of data, capability of team) and the availability of an EPA subject matter expert to work with the team to provide expert knowledge about the domain.

In the simplest terms, the goal of having the Analytics team is to support EPA teams in getting answers to questions that would better enable them to progress the seven key actions of the 2016 State of the Environment Report. This should help teams to become more effective in environmental assessments, environmental enforcement and environmental advocacy work. The Analytics team aims to make it easier for staff to spot patterns and trends in data: reducing the time needed to analyse data should have a benefit to team efficiency. The Analytics team are building the capability to model data: the team has experience in trending and statistics but are building capability in modelling future scenarios to support teams in making the best environmental decisions. Finally, the team will produce new datasets which will be shared as open data via Ireland's open data portal for others to use.

Approached to big data and disinformation strategies in Italy: Case study on the Telecommunications Regulator (AGCOM)

Context

Digital markets and on-line platforms are a fundamental part of today's overall global economy. They are a complex ecosystem, populated by several market actors, embracing all economic and social environments. Digital data is pivotal in this ecosystem and in the platforms' economy, where interactions, transactions, consumption and production are made of or based on digital data and information.

It is now well known that digital data economy poses profound policy concerns in terms of data protection and privacy and of impact on competition and consumer protection. Moreover, sophisticated big data owners, through algorithms, can influence perception of facts and news conveyed by digital intermediaries, having a possible impact on freedom of information and media pluralism. Policy makers and regulators are struggling to understand how to proceed and firstly how to approach the existing economic entanglements and trade-offs between:

- the static and dynamic market value of information and data economy
- the respect of individual and collective fundamental rights (e.g., privacy, competition and media pluralism).

Mostly all sectors and all sector regulators are affected by these phenomena; however, communications and media authorities are usually at the front line on digital policy, as they traditionally regulate communications networks, which are the "backbones" of digital ecosystem, and because very often services provided by digital (platforms) are substitutes of traditional communications, information and audio-visual services.

The Italian Communications and Media Regulatory Authority (*Autorità per le Garanzie nelle Comunicazioni,* AGCOM), established in 1997,[1] operates in this context. It was designed as an independent convergent regulator, in order to tackle the challenges posed by the technology and market dynamics in the communications sector. AGCOM supervises:

- Press, audio-visual and media sectors (including among others, competences and powers on advertising; protection of minors; political communication; copyright protection; assessment of dominant positions in the media sector)
- electronic communications sector (including among others, competences and powers on market analysis and definition of remedies to market power situations; definition of universal service obligations; definition of who is an electronic communication operator by holding a specific register; allocation and assignment of spectrum and numbering resources)
- postal services (including among others, competences and powers on Universal Service and quality of service; price regulation and cost accounting; consumer complaints)
- consumer welfare and interest (including, among others, competences and powers on consumer protection and empowerment; consumers' complaints; setting and monitoring quality of services).

All these markets and socio-economic contexts have been heavily impacted and transformed by digitalisation and new digital technologies. However, the current regulatory framework has not completely adapted to those transformations.

Issues

The current regulatory framework

The existing national (i.e. Italian) and EU legal frameworks for electronic communications and media markets have origin in the analogue era, where regulators' competences and powers were designed to govern completely different markets, business models and transactions. At EU level there has been a progressive adaptation to the digital world, by the recently revised EECC[2] and AVMS[3] Directives, however this review process has been slow, partial and approached by incremental and marginal changes to the old regulatory framework. This approach unavoidably implied problematic path dependency phenomena and the difficult trade-offs between:

- the risk of an unbalanced public intervention, based on an extensive enforcement of the old regulatory model, hampering innovation
- the risk of a lack of intervention, not addressing new market failure issues, not promoting a competitive level playing field among the different layers and/or nodes of the digital ecosystem and not properly protecting consumers' digital rights.

Moreover, the traditional regulatory approach is based on market-specific rationales, whereas today's markets are subject to a "new convergence", following the first one between telco and media, which AGCOM, and other regulators, were designed to tackle. This new convergence is driven by digitalisation and the development of data economy: all different parts of the digital ecosystem are so closely interrelated and make it difficult to identify well-defined relevant markets, whereas the main players are (few) large global companies (e.g., Amazon, Facebook, Google, Apple, Microsoft) characterised by a high degree of vertical and horizontal integration in many segments of the ecosystem, working together with a myriad of small specialised companies.

Finally, current regulatory policies are designed and implemented at a national level (or at continental level), whereas the digital and data economy, the digital platforms and their end-users have global features and attitudes. This unavoidably implies a reduced regulatory capacity, misalignment of incentives and cross-country externalities among the different national public bodies involved. These mismatches are affecting the ability of national public bodies to effectively govern the new markets and new social interactions. This ineffectiveness is also due to an augmented asymmetry of information in the digital world: it is indeed very difficult for public bodies to "push" digital actors to reveal relevant information related both to 1) their internal technical functioning (they are almost "black boxes" from regulators' perspectives); and 2) the global digital market(s) dynamics. Regulators very often do not have tools to fill this deep informational gap.

Digital platforms' business models and economics

The main disruptive aspect of on-line platform economics concerns the establishment of a business model based on global digital transactions, where data is implicitly exchanged for cheap or free services in a multi-sided market context. The other relevant (and potentially disruptive) economic feature of digital platforms is that they can drastically reduce consumers' transaction and search costs, allowing reaching cost-efficient outcomes similar to a perfect competition context. Yet, there is a huge difference. Within digital markets information at the base of such productive efficiency is not a public good, i.e. perfectly observable by everyone, but (*de facto*) internalised and exploited by (vertically and horizontally) integrated platforms. Indeed, the larger platforms are (getting closer to have all possible subscribers and embracing more and more traditional markets) the more efficient their algorithms and their services are. Larger and larger sets of customers' data give platforms the ability to identify preferences and willingness to pay of each customer and thus perfectly discriminate. This also affects the users' incentives to increasingly "trade" data in the implicit exchange for "free" services and to stay inert as consumers, therefore not sanctioning service-providers (and making data portability provisions useless).

What is positive under a productive-efficiency perspective is leading consumers to make their choices in smaller markets, finally tailored on each consumer This phenomenon, jointly with indirect and direct network externalities, make users locked-in an "information digital aftermarket" by gatekeepers which looks like "the market", by selecting each user's services, products and influencing their preferences. This outcome may not well be desirable from a competitive and social point of view, particularly when we consider the information system and informative contents that are able to influence personal and public opinion.

In fact, in the digital ecosystem there is a larger availability of informative contents on the supply side. However, the reduction of transaction and search costs also decreases time that consumers use to information seeking. Digital platforms thus solve the digital information overload and efficiently select relevant information by perfectly discriminating and matching consumers (current) preferences on informative contents. Nevertheless, this unavoidably undermines pluralism, because consumers receive their own world representation, whereas any informative content they might currently disagree with is not selected or offered.

This process has been observed as leading to pathological information phenomena such as confirmation bias, echo chambers and citizen polarisation (i.e. the tendency to acquire mainly information consistent with their ideological preferences) and to disinformation phenomena (such as fake news).

Approach and interventions

AGCOM has planned and implemented a number of regulatory and policy actions to understand and address the digital transformation phenomena focusing on both big data and disinformation strategies, which are strictly interrelated.

AGCOM's vision on a new policy paradigm for big data

Building on its market inquiry about "Internet services and on-line advertising" (published in 2014),[4] AGCOM has started a big data market inquiry (which is part of a joint assessment carried out with the competition and data protection authorities) and in September 2018 published its Interim Report.[5]

AGCOM strongly believes that, because of structural and lasting market failures in digital data markets, it is necessary to adopt an *ex ante* approach to the data regulation (and to possible regulation of related algorithms), while competition law enforcement and data protection are not sufficient. Moreover, since the digital ecosystem is very complex, a holistic/horizontal regulatory approach to its networks and services is necessary: an approach able to look at and address system interdependences, so neither risking to a negative impact on innovation nor to provide an incomplete or merely formal protection of consumers' and citizens' rights. In other words, it is necessary to build a horizontal regulatory framework for digital economy to protect and empower consumers and citizens in all digital ecosystem's markets and segments, where consumers' information and data are crucial.

Within data markets, regulators have a pervasive and structural information asymmetry vis-à-vis operators. As a first step of the new regulatory paradigm, therefore it is necessary to open up the "black box" and look at the complex and composite digital data transaction. Therefore, regulators need to be provided with relevant inspections powers in order to ascertain and assess, among others, timing and methods of data acquisition (data gathering and storage), functioning of the algorithms (algorithm accountability), methods of data conservation and analysis (data analytics), derived information, and deriving (primary and secondary) uses.

Second point is that big data dynamics, jointly with the Internet of Things, Artificial Intelligence and 5G, make it necessary to overcome the traditional distinction between different types of data (personal, non-personal, sensitive, etc.), whereas the new approach must refer simply to the data "per se".

Third, regulators must be given mandate, competences and powers to address or minimise risk of new market failures (such as implicit transactions, incomplete markets, information asymmetries, hold-up and locked-in phenomena) and to disentangle the trade-off between platform efficiency and the informational aftermarkets they create. To do that it is necessary (yet not sufficient) to look at data as an economic good, so focusing on consumers' incentives to engage in transactions and what are the economic effects of those transactions. In this way, it is possible to make the digital data transaction explicit and empower consumers to exercise their (existing) property rights and thus exerting a decentralised discipline on platforms' market and contractual power. Indeed, a key policy issue in the data economy is the definition of entitlements on data property rights, coherent with data protection rules, in order to enable owners to explicitly exchange them in the data market or exclude any other party from accessing or using them – even from "internal use" as profitably done by vertically and horizontally-integrated multi-sided platforms.

This approach would also tackle the existing tension between objectives of data protection and pro-competitive rules, and it must be based on a strict co-ordination/integration of those rules and the implementing bodies. Protecting the digital data privacy but neglecting the implicit exchange of that data in an incomplete (and unregulated) market risk to jeopardise market dynamics, giving platforms incentives to vertically and horizontally integrate in order to internalise the most sides of the data market, and ultimately hamper the final user-consumer. As mentioned, it is crucial to look and regulate data as an economic good, and that is exactly the approach that GDPR, with data portability provisions, and other EU data policies are starting to build.

AGCOM's approach to on-line pluralism ("pluralism 2.0"), fake news and disinformation

Digital platforms today play an increasingly pivotal role in the information system, which has been structurally changed by big data. This is due mainly to the capacity of digital platforms to gather personal information and extract value from data by means of accurate profiling ("data analytics"), which makes these actors the world leaders in the (on-line) advertising sector – a resource that is still the main source of funding for online and off-line information. Moreover, search engines and social networks play an increasingly crucial role as 1) direct information tools, because a large and growing portion of people use social networks to keep up with the news; and 2) distribution channel for online news, provided that they operate as gatekeepers for access and distribution of online contents. Big data is crucial also under a pluralism point of view, as it is at basis of platforms algorithms functions, and allow personalisation of information generation and distribution, and thus disinformation, polarisation and other pathological information phenomena. Within social networks, automatic customisation systems (operating by means of algorithms and big data) and the sharing user-generated informative contents support the viral widespread of polarising contents and the proliferation of fake news.

Online information distortions represent a complex and multifaceted phenomenon, varying in terms of actors involved, underlying motivations, communication techniques, tools and technologies used, and resources invested. To understand this phenomenon, AGCOM has conducted market research on "News consumption" (published in February 2018)[6] and is carrying out a market inquiry on "On-line disinformation strategies and the fake content supply chain" (interim report published in November 2018).[7]

The main outcomes are the following. First, online disinformation distortions operate on both the supply and the demand side of the information system. Secondly, the fake-news production, distribution and dissemination processes hinge on a full-fledged supply chain of fake contents, which may be structured according to promoters' motivations and the kind of audience targeted by the disinformation strategy. Thirdly, it is possible to detect on-line disinformation strategies by exploring each specific case of online disinformation strategy and its supply chain, and AGCOM is doing that by its observatory on online disinformation (see below). Those strategies are characterised by a certain standard number and types of disinformation actions, including an array of publishing and re-publishing fake contents.

Against this variety of online disinformation problems, AGCOM believes that both self-regulatory and (co) regulatory measures should be adopted. With this aim, on November 16, 2017, with its resolution n.423/17/CONS, AGCOM launched a co-regulation "technical committee ('*tavolo tecnico*')" on pluralism and fair information on digital platforms",[8] comprising AGCOM and most of the market stakeholders (e.g. social networks –Facebook–, search engines –Google–, press editors and audio-visual service providers). AGCOM's technical committee aims to create consensus, identify and promote self- and co-regulatory solutions to online disinformation problems. The committee is co-ordinated by AGCOM's directors of the Economic Analysis and AVMS Directorates.

The "technical committee" comprises five working groups, dealing with:

- methodologies for classifying and detecting online disinformation phenomena;
- definition of monitoring systems for economic advertising flows aimed at financing fake content;
- fact-checking: organisation, techniques, tools and effects;
- media and digital literacy;
- design and implementation of information campaigns about disinformation aimed at consumers.

One of most important achievements of the technical committee was the approval of the "Guidelines for equal access to online platforms during the election campaign for the political elections", which identified a few goals in view of the last national political elections, that the stakeholders involved committed to comply with:

- Equity of access to all political subjects to the information and political communication tools offered by digital platforms
- Transparency of political advertisements
- Ban of illegal content (i.d. defamatory content against candidates or the circulation of opinion polls in the last15 days before the elections)
- Improvement of the fact-checking activities

In 2019, a new set of Guidelines was approved, and it contained a more detailed set of commitments, drafted on the basis of the commitments established by the EU Code of Practice against disinformation.

The pluralism committee, and the related co-regulation approach, is another way to open up the "black box", by means of analysis and surveys based on information provided by online platforms. With this approach, AGCOM's is looking at the techniques of newsfeed and algorithmic selection, editorial framing and organisation, stakeholders' transparency policy for users.

AGCOM's pluralism committee is working to establish operative solutions, among which there are:

- Constant monitoring of online disinformation and hate speech phenomena, by establishing the observatory on online disinformation: the observatory first report was published in March 2019.[9]
- Establishing a co-ordination platform for autonomous fact-checking activities and setting journalistic standards in terms of transparency, ethics and quality of the editorial structure.
- Actions for media literacy and against online hate speech phenomena: a draft regulation on hate speech was published in 2019.[10]
- Definition and implementation of direct access procedures – by a third independent party – to profiled data, in order to assess the impact of self and co-regulatory measures.

Results, impact and lessons learnt

Main result of AGCOM's actions about big data and disinformation strategies was to partially open-up the "black box" and partially fill the informational gap. This has been done by means of:

- market inquiries, often carried out in co-operation with other public bodies (e.g., competition authority, data protection authority, governmental agency for cybersecurity and PA digitalisation)
- studies and specific research commissioned to universities and research centres
- co-operation with market actors and stakeholders (technical committee on pluralism and disinformation, adoption of self and co-regulation approaches based on data provided by the market).

These activities also allowed AGCOM:

- to promote the adaptation of platforms governance and self-regulation in a number of contexts, particularly related to disinformation strategies and "hate speech"
- to identify contexts where the current legal frameworks, regulatory mandates and powers are not completely adequate
- promoting large information campaigns to effectively increase consumers/citizens' information and attention on those issues.

AGCOM's inquiries and dissemination activities has also fed public policy debates on the adaptation of public intervention to ongoing digital transformations of markets and society, both in terms of revision of current regulatory frameworks ("digital update"), and also in terms of institutional design (i.e. the establishment of an "horizontal" Authority competent for all the regulatory issues in the digital markets, proposal echoed somehow in a number of other countries, such as UK, France, Australia and Japan).

There is now an increased awareness in the public opinion about the impact of digital and data economy. National (and continental) policy makers well understand that it is fundamental to assess the impact of digitalisation and disruptive technologies on regulatory capacity of national public bodies, with the aim to understand if and how re-think and re-define regulators' competences, powers and co-operative mechanisms both to facilitate the development and exploitation of the digital and data economy potential benefits, and to address also its challenges and risks.

Co-operation

AGCOM has established several co-operation agreements and Memoranda of Understanding with other Italian regulators and institutions whose competencies are adjacent or anyhow related to AGCOM's remit. The full list of agreements is available (in Italian) at this page: https://www.agcom.it/accordi-di-collaborazione. It is worthwhile mentioning the MoUs in place with the National Competition Authority (AGCM),[11] with the energy, gas and water regulator[12] (ARERA) and with the transport regulator (ART),[13] all established on 2016. Other specific co-operation activities are put in place with the aim of carry out joint activities and achieve specific goals on areas of common interest; this is the case of the above mentioned joint investigation by AGCOM, AGCM and the Data Protection Body on Big Data. Another example of targeted co-operation experience is between AGCOM and ARERA on the issue of IoT and M2M technologies. In addition, on administrative matters, national legislative provisions request that national regulators exploit some synergies in carrying out jointly human resources hiring procedures or hardware and IT procurement procedures.

The international co-operation commitments of AGCOM are grounded on different bases: first, it is worth mentioning the co-operation within sectoral regulatory bodies (i.e. BEREC, ERGA, ERGP, RSPG) based on the provisions of the *Acquis Communautaire* and aimed at fostering the exchange of best practices among NRAS and supporting the EU Commission in the development of its tasks. Other co-operation fora are in place within sectoral regional platforms of regulators (EMERG, EPRA, ReseauMed), as well as within the activities of international organisations (OECD, ITU).

Last, AGCOM has a long-standing score of bilateral co-operation with other NRAs/institutions, on the asis of EU funded projects (Twinning or TAIEX Projects) and of bilateral Memorandum of Understanding.

Notes

[1] Law No. 249/1997 of the Italian Parliament.

[2] The Directive (EU) 2018/1972 of 11 December 2018 establishing the European Electronic Communications Code (Recast) is available at: https://eur-lex.europa.eu/legal-content/en/txt/?uri=celex:32018l1972.

[3] The latest review of AVMSD, Directive (EU) 2018/1808, has been completed on 6 November 2018. Revised AVMS Directive, is available at: https://eur-lex.europa.eu/eli/dir/2018/1808/oj The description of the latest review is available at: https://ec.europa.eu/digital-single-market/en/revision-audiovisual-media-services-directive-avmsd.

[4] AGCOM, 2019, "INDAGINE CONOSCITIVA SUL SETTORE DEI SERVIZI INTERNET E

SULLA PUBBLICITÀ ONLINE" [Knowledge survery on the internet services sector and online advertising], https://www.agcom.it/documents/10179/540203/Allegato+21-01-2014+2/9376a211-ebb2-4df6-83ea-282f731faaf2?version=1.1.

[5] AGCOM, 2017, Interim report in the context of the joint inquiry on "Big data" launched by the AGCOM deliberation No. 217/17 / CONS, https://www.agcom.it/documents/10179/11898202/Studio-Ricerca+04-09-2018/388e9d5d-e80f-4af4-a017-b81615c41fc1?version=1.0.

[6] AGCOM, 2018, Report on the news consumption, https://www.agcom.it/documents/10179/10214149/Studio-Ricerca+10-04-2018/4619854b-6d9b-491b-a3c8-f7444487006d?version=1.0.

[7] AGCOM, 2018, News v Fake in the information system - Interim report, https://www.agcom.it/documents/10179/12791486/Allegato+25-1-2019/831ee043-55dd-41e2-b87d-4578016b9989?version=1.0.

[8] AGCOM, 2018, Tavolo pluralismo e piattaforme online [Pluralism table and online platforms],

https://www.agcom.it/tavolo-pluralismo-e-piattaforme-online.

[9] AGCOM, 2019, Online disinformation monitoring system, https://www.agcom.it/documents/10179/14174124/Allegato+12-3-2019/679c5e28-5a99-4d1b-b638-1a04e2c63c18?version=1.0.

[10] AGCOM, 2019, Consultazione pubblica sullo schema di regolamento recante disposizioni in materia di rispetto della dignità umana e del principio di non discriminazione e di contrasto all'hate speech

[Public consultation on the draft regulation containing provisions on respect for human dignity and the principle of non-discrimination and contrast to hate speech] https://www.agcom.it/documents/10179/13446572/delibera+25-19-cons/9e06b04c-9a35-40de-88d2-62f2580dc25d?version=1.0.

[11] AGCOM, 2017, Protocollo d'Intesa Agcom-Agcm su pratiche commerciali scorrette 22 dicembre 2016 [Agcom-Agcm Memorandum of Understanding on unfair commercial practices 22 December 2016] https://www.agcom.it/documentazione/documento?p_p_auth=flw7zrht&p_p_id=101_instance_fnow5lvoix oe&p_p_lifecycle=0&p_p_col_id=column-1&p_p_col_count=1&_101_instance_fnow5lvoixoe_struts_action=%2fasset_publisher%2fview_content&_101_instance_fnow5lvoixoe_assetentryid=6765146&_101_instance_fnow5lvoixoe_type=document.

[12] AGCOM, 2016, *Protocollo di intesa tra l'Autorità per l'energia elettrica il gas e il sistema idrico e l'Autorità per le garanzie nelle comunicazioni* [Memorandum of Understanding between the Authority for Electricity, Gas and the Water System and the Authority for Communications Guarantees] https://www.agcom.it/documentazione/documento?p_p_auth=flw7zrht&p_p_id=101_instance_fnow5lvoix oe&p_p_lifecycle=0&p_p_col_id=column-1&p_p_col_count=1&_101_instance_fnow5lvoixoe_struts_action=%2fasset_publisher%2fview_content&_101_instance_fnow5lvoixoe_assetentryid=4659736&_101_instance_fnow5lvoixoe_type=document.

[13] AGCOM, 2016, *Protocollo di intesa tra l'Autorità di regolazione dei trasporti e l'Autorità per le garanzie nelle comunicazioni* [Memorandum of Understanding between the Transport Regulatory Authority and the Authority for Communications Guarantees] https://www.agcom.it/documentazione/documento?p_p_auth=flw7zrht&p_p_id=101_instance_fnow5lvoix oe&p_p_lifecycle=0&p_p_col_id=column-1&p_p_col_count=1&_101_instance_fnow5lvoixoe_struts_action=%2fasset_publisher%2fview_content&_101_instance_fnow5lvoixoe_assetentryid=6452760&_101_instance_fnow5lvoixoe_type=document.

Regulation of non-scheduled road transport passenger services in Italy: Case study on the Transport Regulation Authority (ART)

The text below reproduces verbatim the translation in English of a recommendation (*atto di segnalazione*) that the Italian Transport Regulation Authority addressed to Parliament and Government in 2015 as a result of its monitoring of the evolution of the markets for non-scheduled road transport passenger services, and in the context of emerging transformations on both the demand and supply sides thereof.[1]

Notably, the recommendation was adopted before the EU Court of Justice ruled, in 2017 and 2018, on relevant cases concerning the operation of the company UBER, respectively, in Spain and France.

Based on ongoing observation of the market and on its experience in dealing with a number of dossiers in this area, the update of the document is in progress at the time of writing.

Purpose, object and structure

The recent widespread use of information technologies applied in an innovative way to passenger mobility has had significant effects on both users' demand and behaviour and the availability of non-scheduled local transport services, highlighting that it would be appropriate to regulate the technology platforms that mediate between supply and demand (herein referred to as "technology mobility services" or TMS) and remove some of the constraints associated with the provision of taxi and car and driver hire (hereinafter C&DH) services. In this regard the Italian Transport Regulation Authority (hereinafter the Authority) wishes to provide initial indications for the purpose of promoting competition and ensuring adequate levels of quality and efficiency for non-scheduled road transport passenger services.

The proposals described below were approved by the Board of the Authority at its meeting on 21 May 2015 in the discharge of its functions of reporting to the Government and the Parliament on the evolution of the transport sector and the legislative amendments which may consequently be required. The reporting activity is based on article 37, paragraph 2, letter m) of Decree-Law No. 201 of 6 December 2011, converted, after amendments, by Law No. 214 of 21 December 2011, establishing the Transport Regulation Authority and on article 2, paragraphs 6 and 12, of Law No. 481 of 14 November 1995 providing "Rules relating to competition and the regulation of public utility services. Establishment of regulatory authorities for public utility services".

The proposed legislative changes resulting from the Authority's indications relate exclusively to Law No. 21 of 15 January 1992 ("Framework law on non-scheduled public road passenger transport services"). If accepted, the related set of rules should also be amended. Further, the above provisions setting up the Authority should be revised with particular reference to the following functions and activities:

- definition of the criteria for taxi fare setting
- adoption of measures aimed at ensuring that the levels of taxi service supply and the quality of the service provision correspond to the mobility needs of the travelling public
- monitoring of dynamic tariff adjustment mechanisms (so-called *surge pricing*) used by TMS and possible intervention with appropriate regulatory measures (including containment)
- provision of an adequate transitional system which ensures the compliance with the current quotas in the first phase of implementation.

This document is accompanied by drafts of legislative proposals (Encl. 1) and a table comparing the current regulation and the regulation that would result from the adoption of the Authority's proposals (Encl. 2).

Regulatory framework and new regulatory requirements

The above-mentioned Law No. 21 of 1992 provides the regulatory framework governing taxi and C&DH services devolving the establishment of detailed rules and rules concerning the management of such services to regions and local authorities. Significant differences characterise the arrangements for market access in the two cases. Both services provide collective or individual passenger transport services, additional and complementary to scheduled public passenger transport services; both services are provided at the request of passengers, on an occasional or periodic basis, for a given duration and/or itinerary (article 1, paragraph 1). However, while C&DH services are not subject to public service obligations, taxi services fall very clearly into the category of local public transport services, albeit non-scheduled.

The public nature of the service implies mandatory performance, territorial and social coverage of the service provision and economic accessibility of the taxi service. The nature of the service, beside its mandatory performance, implies undifferentiated provision to any requesting passenger, strict public determination of service fares and procedures, parking of the vehicle used as a taxi in a public place and collection of the user or beginning of the service to take place within the municipal or district area.

The geographical nature of the service organisation markedly characterises the current regulation. By implementing Law No. 21 of 1992, the regions identify the criteria to be observed by municipalities when drafting their regulations governing the provision of non-scheduled public road transport passenger services and devolve the administrative duties relating to their enforcement to local authorities. Municipalities, in turn, regulate the fees required for the service, the number of individual operators, the daily shifts, working hours, rules of conduct and safety conditions. Thus, when establishing the regulations governing the provision of non-scheduled public road passenger transport services, the municipalities shall specify: number and type of vehicles to be assigned to each service; procedures for the provision of the service; criteria for taxi fare setting; requirements and conditions for the grant of a license to operate a taxi service.

On the economic level and in terms of domestic market structure, the processing of data concerning ten regional capitals, directly provided by municipalities and those contained in the 2006 and 2014 Annual Reports of the *Agenzia per il controllo e la qualità dei servizi pubblici locali di Roma Capitale* (the Agency for monitoring and quality of local public services of Roma Capitale) reveals that the number of taxis in recent years remained substantially unchanged. With regard to taxi fares, the maximum rates are usually approved by the municipalities concerned and no price discount or customer retention policies are provided, except in rare cases. As for the structure, the fare consists of an initial fixed amount (EUR 2-3) and a minimum amount for each journey. Two other components are added: the first depending on dwell time or routes travelled below a certain speed (EUR 20-30 per hour) and a second component depending on the kilometres travelled (EUR 0.7 to 1.15 per km). The latter, in large Italian cities (Rome, Milan, Turin and Florence), increases with longer routes. The basic fare is supplemented by extra fares for night service (EUR 2-3.5), holiday service (EUR 1.5-2.5), radio-taxi service (EUR 0.6 to 3.5), for each baggage (EUR 0.3-1), number of passengers in excess of three, transport of small domestic animals, transport of skis, etc. In addition, fixed rates are charged for certain connections, typically to and from the airport. With regard to the fare dynamics, in recent years sample cities have recorded increases usually higher than inflation. For example, between 2006 and 2014, compared to an average price increase of 15% (source: ISTAT, the Italian Institute of Statistics), rates increased by 37% in Rome, 29% in Florence and 23% in Milan.

Moreover, while the fare levels do not seem related to the ratio between number of taxis and population density, there is, however, a positive correlation between fares and average income of resident population, indicating that the taxi service meets mainly the needs of certain segments of the non-scheduled local transport market: in particular, the demand of the population with upper-middle income, business users and, in part, that related to tourism. In this market segment, the complex nature of the fare, the different combination of its components and the amounts varying from city to city do not allow an advance estimate of the fare.

Against this background, Italy – as many other countries – is witnessing an increased use of technology platforms that provide TMS and allow to connect passengers, vehicles and drivers even outside the areas covered by current regulation (taxi and C&DH). While taxi and C&DH services meet a part of the mobility demand left unsatisfied by scheduled public transport, there are also systems based on the flexibility and sharing of resources attributable to the so-called sharing economy. These include both key enablers, such as TMS, and other innovative mobility systems, including bike sharing, car sharing and carpooling. With respect to these new systems, the widespread dissemination of highly competitive mobile technologies allowed to activate specific online and mobile service platforms that interconnect demand and supply of services and, thanks to geo-localisation, identify and make available on demand the closest vehicles and other transport mobility means.

On the whole, these systems have significant effects on the supply of non-scheduled road transport passenger services; in particular, the TMS intercept a demand for services which are typically less expensive than those provided by taxi and C&DH and are available with different delivery modes. This points towards the creation of a new and specific segment of the non-scheduled urban mobility market other than that subject to public service obligations. In a wide-ranging policy perspective, it fits in with the development of sustainable "co-modal" and "technology-based" mobility systems and the pursuit of indirect deflation effects as for circulation and pollution reduction. Its diffusion requires to re-examine whether the current legal institutions and categories regulating this subject-matter are still satisfactory.

The Authority's survey: The complementary nature of regulated services and services provided through the use of new technologies

Within the above framework, the Authority considered it appropriate to carry out a survey aimed at expanding on the knowledge and understanding of the above-mentioned services, their trends and implications in terms of economic regulation. All the major stakeholders were involved: associations representing taxi and C&DH service operators, new technology platforms operating in different ways in this sector, consumer groups, the National Association of Italian Municipalities (ANCI) and the Conference of the Regions and autonomous Provinces.

The survey highlighted the exponential growth in the last twelve months in the number of non-professional drivers registered on the platforms providing TMS and the corresponding increase in the number of registered users and journeys. With respect to fares, in some cases, the price of the journey is exclusively proportional, in whole or in part, to the "living expenses" incurred by the driver. In other cases, it covers other business costs. Other cases involve the application of dynamic tariff adjustment mechanisms (the so-called surge pricing) which is widespread in other transport sectors and requires a specific focus.

Based on the outcome of the Authority's survey, a general consensus was reached on the need to protect users with respect to the safety and quality of the services and the privacy of passengers. On the other hand, different approaches were taken into consideration as regards the Government intervention on the new platforms through authoritative and regulatory measures, also for the purposes of removing some of the current restrictions to market access and provision of services. In particular, it was pointed out that the regulation should orderly enhance the different ways of satisfying the mobility demand and support market segmentation, thereby reducing the risk of distortions.

Taking, for example, carpooling, which consists in sharing a private car between a group of people to cover a route chosen by the driver at a price that allows exclusively to help cover its variable costs, it is necessary that regulation ensures both the functionality of the system vis-à-vis the objective of containing the negative externalities arising from the new approach in the mobility demand and the nature and purpose of the formula, which must not serve a business purpose and must not constitute a market with competing services.

The evidence gathered during the survey points to the need to promote with appropriate regulation the development of the supply of a number of road transport passenger services, to match the new segmentation of urban mobility demand produced by suitable and competitive mobile technologies and by the resulting change in users' consumption habits. The aim is to enhance this new market so that demand and supply of services can operate in a transparent manner and in compliance with the schemes governing business activities.

Not only is this not self-contradictory, but indeed requires the maintenance and development of the transport market activities characterised by public service obligations, which should be made more efficient and, where possible, developed with innovative forms of supply and delivery.

The Authority's proposals

Moving from the foregoing considerations, the Authority wishes to supply some guidance on the economic and regulatory aspects of non-scheduled road transport passenger services and submit such information to the Government and Parliament so that it can be taken into account when defining the policy objectives concerning, *inter alia*, public order and civil and tax regulations, that exceed the Authority's remit.

The indications are briefly described here below and are reflected in proposals for legislative changes. They have been developed taking into account the existing legislation in support of shared transport systems,[2] as well as recent legislative proposals in this field.[3]

In the first place, the proposals move from the assumption that taxi public services retain the current features ensuring the operation of the journey upon request and the provision of the service throughout the day. Taxi services are characterised as public services on the basis of the following requirements:

- identifiable vehicle
- remuneration at regulated prices
- free-of-charge access to equipped parking lots on public land and limited traffic zones and right to use dedicated bus lanes in urban centres
- rebates on fuel excise duties
- and any other benefits and incentives adopted by the legislature.

Furthermore, it is proposed to remove the constraints that currently prevent taxi license holders from granting discounts, making it possible to offer a wider range of services and promoting an increase in demand.

It would be also advisable to modify the legal form of the taxi driver activity in the country, which, unlike C&DH services, is currently excluded from the business activity and therefore should be regulated accordingly. This should be accompanied by the removal of the ban that prevents the enterprise operating taxi services from accumulating a number of licenses. Furthermore, the use of taxi services could be expanded, at least on an experimental basis and in return for adequate compensation, for the purpose of delivering flexible public services for targeted users or adduction to public transport lines where demand is weaker (for example, due to nature of the territory or certain time slots). In addition, it would seem necessary to implement the criterion referred to in Article 37, paragraph 2.2, letter m) of Decree-Law No. 201 of 6 December 2011 and allow license holders greater freedom in the service organisation, both to address with flexible shifts specific extraordinary events or periods of expected increase in demand, and develop new integrated services such as the collective use of taxis.

Finally, it is necessary to remove the existing constraints in certain municipal regulations and contractual acts of radio-taxi management services which require their members to acquire taxi rides only through reference co-operatives or consortiums and prohibit the simultaneous use of other radio-taxis or innovative systems not related to traditional radio stations. In this respect, also in consideration of the public service nature of the service provided by taxi drivers, these provisions which limit the matching of supply and demand are considered as unduly restricting competition, with negative impact on the users. For this reason, it is proposed to declare the invalidity of such provisions and consequently revise the rules contained in municipal regulations or in regional legislation that prevent taxi drivers from acquiring services from different and competing sources. Thus, it would be affirmed that the holder of a license to operate a taxi service or an authorisation to operate a C&DH service can freely acquire rides offered by any radio-taxi or technology platform (see below). The provision should be applied also to the license holders' substitutes.

As for C&DH services, the Authority agrees on the need – already underlined by the Competition Authority – to reduce the differences among the various non-scheduled transport services to increase competition between taxi services and C&DH services and also reduce environmental costs. For this purpose it is proposed to lift the obligation providing that the holder of an authorisation to operate a C&DH service must return to the garage after each service, since this constraint is limiting the economic and efficient performance of this activity.

The revision of the concept of "territoriality" is of paramount importance. In this respect it is suggested to entrust regions with the identification of the ideal areas for taxi and C&DH services management on the basis of the economic, cultural and tourist characteristics of the territories, as well as the administrative functions for the establishment of the number of cars. Essentially, the scope of the service management currently hinged on municipal areas should be expanded. The proposal is completed by providing that regions conclude mutual agreements for the inter-regional operation of taxi and C&DH services.

On the other hand, in the proposed approach, some emerging non-scheduled transport formulas – other than taxi and C&DH services – are subject to obligations which are totally new for them and relate to the service quality and safety. To this end, it is necessary to distinguish two cases in the aforementioned carpooling formula:

- On the one hand, platforms promoting forms of shared transport services of a non-commercial, "courtesy" nature, provided in a non-professional manner by drivers who share, in whole or in part, a predetermined route travelled with their own vehicle, with one or more other persons who get in touch through dedicated services provided by intermediaries through technological tools.

- On the other hand, platforms offering technology intermediation services on demand and for commercial purposes. In the latter case, even if the driver's activities are carried out in an unprofessional manner, the service is provided at a price that does not merely covers (or rather, shares) the cost of the travelled route, defined at the passenger's request, but also ensures a profit margin to platform and driver, albeit at an affordable cost.

- Besides operating conditions to be made subject to provisions for law & order, and civil and tax purposes, with respect to the proposed approach and regulatory objectives, the commercial nature of the transport service should involve specific obligations related to intermediation services and driver's requirements. These obligations should not be imposed on non-commercial, "courtesy" services. In particular:

  - "Intermediaries" could be defined those undertakings providing TMS which, through the use of a technology platform, connect passengers and drivers so as to provide on request a paid-for transport service in the national territory. Intermediaries are registered in the regions that, given the estimated intermunicipal – if not also inter-regional – nature of the service, should also carry out the related administrative functions, directly or through a delegated entity.

o   Several people may be qualified as "drivers": holders of a license to operate a taxi service, holders of an authorisation to operate a C&DH service and private drivers using their own private vehicle. In the latter case, the private driver should be a casual worker, required to comply with a maximum annual income and a limited weekly working time not exceeding fifteen hours (while shifts of professional drivers can reach twelve hours daily). All drivers should be enrolled in a special register established on a regional basis.

Notes

[1] The English courtesy translation of the recommendation is available at the following internet address: https://www.autorita-trasporti.it/atti-di-segnalazione/recommendation-to-the-italian-government-and-parliament-non-scheduled-road-transport-passenger-services-taxi-car-and-driver-hire-and-technology-mobility-services/?lang=en. The Italian original version is complemented by a set of proposals for amending existing legislation, which are not reproduced here.

[2] Article 22, paragraph 1 of Law No. 340 of 24 November 2000 on "Measures for deregulation and simplification of administrative procedures – so-called Simplification Law 1999" refers to the carpooling among the instruments of Urban Mobility Plans of local governments. Similarly, article 2, paragraph 7 of the Decree of the Ministry of Environment of 3 August 2007 on "Funding programme for air quality improvement in urban areas and public transport strengthening", mentions the carpooling among the services ancillary to local public transport and worthy of specific public financing measures. In the same way, article 6, paragraph 1, letter l of Ministerial Decree of 1 February 2013 of the Ministry of Infrastructure and Transport on measures for "Deployment of Intelligent Transport Systems (ITS) in Italy", transposing Directive 2010/40/EU on the deployment of intelligent transport systems into national legislation, urges local authorities to encourage the deployment of carpooling among the smart mobility systems in urban centres.

[3] See Draft Law – Dell'Orco and others: "Amendments to Article 23 of Decree Law No. 83 of 22 June 2012, converted, with amendments, by Law No. 134 of 7 August 2012 and other measures to promote the shared use of private vehicles" (Chamber of Deputies Act 2436).

Supervising electricity and mining companies with drones and virtual reality in Peru: Case study on the Energy and Mining Regulator (Osinergmin)

Institution and relevant market/context information

Osinergmin (*Organismo Supervisor de la Inversión en Energía y Minería*) is the economic regulatory and infrastructure safety supervisor for the energy and mining sectors. In the electricity sector, Osinergmin supervises the compliance with regulations dealing with the generation, the transmission and the distribution of electrical energy. It also oversees the fulfilment of concession contracts in relation to these activities. More particularly the department in charge of supervising compliance with regulations and obligations imposed by concession contracts is the *División de Supervisión de Electricidad* (DSE).

In the mining sector, Osinergmin supervises compliance with technical regulations relating to mining infrastructure, installations and safety of operations for medium[1] and large[2] mining companies. These regulations include, for instance, the state of geo-technical structures, ventilation and transport vehicles. The department in charge of supervising these activities is the *Gerencia de Supervisión Minera* (GSM).

Osinergmin supervises 172 mining operation sites; it also supervises the infrastructure of 57 electricity generation companies, 18 transmission companies and 20 distribution companies. These facilities are located all around the country; many of them are located in remote areas that are difficult to access.

To fulfill its supervising functions, Osinergmin needs information regarding the facilities. Regulations vest Osinergmin with inspection and sanctioning powers. Information and evidence are collected at the occasion of site visits and are included in supervision reports. Corrective or preventive measures are taken in case the supervisors find evidence of breach of regulations.

Problem

Supervising electrical and mining facilities is complicated and risky. It is sometimes logistically difficult to perform the assessment of electrical and mining infrastructures. For instance, insufficient time can be a constraint: transmission lines are often very long and it generally takes a lot of time to inspect them (it takes on average eight hours to supervise one kilometre of a transmission line). In consequence, it happens that the supervision personnel cannot perform in practice an exhaustive control of a specific electrical infrastructure site due to time restrictions. In addition, topographical and weather conditions can make supervision activities risky as it happened for instance during the climate pattern known as "El Niño", where heavy rains caused rivers flood.

The collection of visual material, such as photographs and videos, is very helpful for supervisors to complete reports and significantly improves the quality of supervision activities. However, this collection takes time and requires abundant resources. In addition, once the personnel leaves the site, it is very expensive to go back and gather any additional information.

In mining sites, the supervision process requires gathering detailed information about the land surface. Conventional mining supervision is based on topography techniques that often generate unreliable information or poorly detailed information of mining geotechnical components. This problem is particularly frequent on tailing dams and rough mountain terrains in which access is difficult.

Not getting the detailed data might undermine the supervision work and imply risk for mining operations and an increased risk of disaster for people living in the influence area of the mining site as well as for the environment.

Approach and intervention

In order to deal with the above-mentioned challenges and to improve the supervision processes and outcomes, Osinergmin relies on two technological tools that facilitate the work of supervisors in particular in places that are difficult to reach or under dangerous conditions. These tools allow supervisors to significantly increase the availability of image and video without increasing the time allocated to collect them. This substantially diminishes the number of staff hours needed to complete a supervision in locations where access is difficult. Another additional benefit is to reduce risks taken by personnel, increasing safety.

The first tool is the use of drones gathering data. This pilot project was initiated in 2016. The information collected thanks to this tool enables Osinergmin to:

- Monitor critical infrastructure.
- Reduce up to more than 50% the effective average supervision times, covering multiple facilities and components inspected and reduce the number of inspection brigades Get access to high quality images from every angle while keeping supervisors safe.
- Record and review images that can be added to the supervision file in order to decide what actions must be taken to guarantee the quality of the electricity service.

For mining infrastructure, the information collected by drones enables Osinergmin to:

- Create images of the infrastructure for analysing its condition and storing historical information of that component to evaluate relevant changes over time.
- Verify whether topographic parameters are within the requirements set by the ministry of mining.
- Create 3D models to test technical parameters and run stress scenario simulation for infrastructure failure.

The second tool is a pilot project to use drones equipped with a 360° HD video recording equipment and a video processing software to produce virtual reality tour of the supervised infrastructure. The combination of these two technologies enable the supervisors:

- To have a complete record from every point of view of the infrastructure and to redisplay the visit, at the supervisor´s will, from the desired angle, and focus on any detail of the infrastructure.
- To have on-line access to the information and redisplay the visit using a cellular application.

Results, impact and lessons learnt

Gathering data for electricity facilities supervision using drones and virtual reality has proved to be an effective innovation. Thanks to it, Osinergmin now has access to high precision data to evaluate the condition of the infrastructure component. Virtual reality data has added the possibility to display on demand the supervision visit and to focus on details that might had not taken into account during the site supervision visit.

The results obtained thanks to the use of drones were:

- A reduction of the time spent on the site supervision: with the conventional supervision process, it took on average 8 hours to supervise one kilometer of a transmission line (considering a buffer of 50 meters). Since the drones were introduced, it takes about 2 hours at most to supervise 6 kilometers of a transmission line (and the buffer supervised can be expended up to 2 kilometres).

- An increase of capacities to detect failures and imperfections: Some of them cannot be detected with the conventional supervision process but can be detected with drones.

- Access to restricted areas as result of the climate pattern ("El Niño"). The use of drones allowed to identify 50 possible risk situations, which could not be possible to identify without the drones, because it involves a dangerous situation to the supervisors.

- A reduction of the average supervision costs from USD 820 to USD 380.

The results obtained thanks to the use of virtual reality technology were:

- An increase in the volume and the quality of the information about the supervised infrastructure, and the possibility to display on demand the supervision visit on a cellphone.

- A reduction of the time spent on the site supervision. With the conventional supervision process, it took 18 days to supervise 44 aerogenerators, one electrical substation and 12 transmission line structures. Since virtual reality was introduced, it takes about 2 days at most.

- A reduction of the average supervision costs from USD 5 802 to USD 5 268.

As a result, duration and monetary cost of the supervision activities are reduced. Indeed, the quality of service for citizens and industries improved.

For mining supervision gathering data using drones has also proved to be an effective innovation. Thanks to it, Osinergmin now has access to high precision data to evaluate the condition of the infrastructure component. Photogrammetry data has improved the supervision process and outcomes. As a result, Osinergmin can timely take the appropriate measures to ensure the compliance of mining regulations.

Most of the supervision activities that Osinergmin realises are done by contractors. So far, Osinergmin has contracted regular supervision activities with standard technology and, separately, it has contracted specialised companies to gather information with drones. Then, Osinergmin has co-ordinated the supervision processes of both companies.

Osinergmin is considering two approaches to fully integrate drone and 360° HD video recording equipment and video processing software into its regular supervision procedures.

The first approach is to keep separate contractors for drone and 360° HD video recording equipment and video processing software and for supervision activities that use that information as an input. This approach has the advantage of exploiting the comparative advantages of drone companies and supervision activities companies.

The second approach is to bundle both services, making compulsory for supervision contractors to have – or subcontract –drone and 360° HD video recording capabilities. This approach has the advantage of having a single contractor to interact with, but it compels the supervision activities contractor to have or hire drone and 360° HD video recording equipment and video processing software capabilities.

Notes

[1] Mining sites capable of processing between 350 and 5 000 tons per day, or companies whose operation are limited to prospecting activities, extraction of non-metallic minerals or storage of mineral concentrate.

[2] Mining sites capable of processing more than 5 000 tons per day.

Annex 2.C. Osinergmin Peru

Application that provides guidance regarding electrical risks and minimum safety distances in transmission lines. It will be available in Spanish, Aymara and Quechua.

Annex Figure 2.C.1. App with Augmented Reality: Electrical Risks in transmission lines (Data collection)

Use of drones for geotechnical supervision of open pits, tailings deposits, waste deposits and leach piles (2019 Supervision Plan). Information is obtained through the generation of 3D digital models of the physical conditions of the monitored components and the terrain's topography, with greater precision.

Annex Figure 2.C.2. Use of Drones and 3D Digital Models in the Mining Supervision (GSM) process (Data collection)

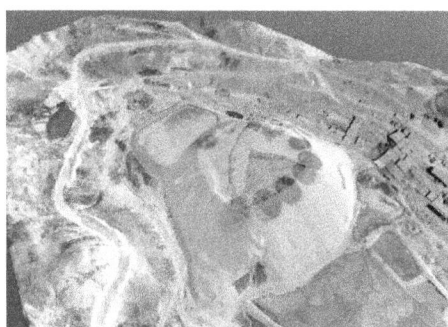

Elevation 3D Digital Model
Huancapetí

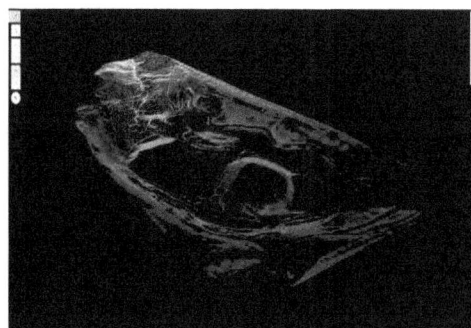

3D Contour Lines
Huancapetí

Digitalisation of processes and regulatory delivery in the Peruvian telecommunications sector: Case study on the Telecommunications Regulator (OSIPTEL)

Context

OSIPTEL (*Organismo Supervisor de Inversión Privada en Telecomunicaciones*) is one of four economic regulators under the aegis of the Presidency of the Council of Ministers, created in the 1990s to oversee Peru's transition to a liberalised economy.[1] It is a specialised and decentralised regulatory body with technical, administrative, economic and financial autonomy in charge of the regulation of Peruvian telecommunications' markets.

Its functions are:

- to set tariffs for public utilities in the telecommunications sector
- to establish norms and rules
- to supervise compliance with legal framework
- to enforce regulations
- to act as second instance for customer claims
- to act as competition agency for telecommunication market.

The telecommunications industry is characterised by its technological dynamism. This constant change promotes the existence of new services, upgrades on existing services as well as more efficiency on markets. In particular, wireless technologies have become an inflexion point on the deployment of networks, which allows for increased coverage and access.

In Peru, mobile phone access went from 35% of total households to more than 95% at a national level (70% in rural areas) between 2014 and 2019. In addition, the number of mobile phone lines went from nearly 3 million to more than 40 million and the traffic increased from nearly 45 billion to more than 70 billion minutes in the same period. Mobile internet started in 2010 and nowadays is the preferred service. Investment registered an increase of more than USD 1 billion between 2014 and 2018. Internet usage increased fourteen-fold between 2014 and 2018. Traffic and number of calls have also increased.

Not surprisingly, the rates for these services have decreased. Mobile phone rates went from more than 35 cents a minute in 2014 to nearly 6 cents these days. As for Internet, the cost for a megabyte went from more than 10 soles to 10 cents on the same period. Industry income has also increased the last four years but at lower rate.

Nevertheless, some remarks have to be made:

- Market structure has changed (the fixed market dropped its market share from 11% to 4% and mobile equipment rose from 8% to 16%).
- The average revenue per user (ARPU) keeps diminishing (on fixed internet from 85 soles to 68 soles and on mobile voice services from 23 soles to 17 soles between 2014 and 2018).
- Income distributes between more competitors (the main two operators went to hold from around 90% of the industry income to 70%).

- Telecommunications have already been deployed to the most profitable areas and the very large majority of households have some type of telecommunication service. In turn, the firms operate in a scarcer telecommunication environment. The challenge they face include:
- It is difficult to reach people and areas that do not have yet access to the telecommunication services (far from the cities, less accessible and low-density areas).
- Deployment costs on uncovered areas are remarkably higher.
- Income and operation margins have decreased.
- It is difficult to get authorisations for deployment of infrastructure.
- Existent capacity is almost completely used and users are not faithful to a brand.

Issues

All these changes, which have taken place over the last four years, added a lot of complexity to the industry and to the role played by the regulator. Communication technologies are part of consumers' everyday life, and they even govern some aspects of their life. In addition, consumers know more about technologies and their uses. As a result, they have become more demanding and meeting this demand has become more complex for the market and the regulator. In particular, the Peruvian telecommunications regulator faces decreasing income (result of more competition on markets) and more requirements for consumers who demand that the government (regulator) guarantees the meeting of their expectations on services.

Even thought, OSIPTEL do have the power, legal framework and functions to face this new context, management's capacities could fail short, considering restrictions on economic resources and lack of agility because of legal constraints for public entities. Actually, we had Therefore, the soon we implement improvements on process in spite of the mentioned limitations, the better, since we would have more degrees of freedom to face upcoming challenges.

In this context, regulators must define a strategy to face the following challenges:

- Gaining speed and flexibility to meet the expectations of the public.
- Achieving their goals of promoting competition, quality on telecommunication services, good consumer services' and telecommunications' markets development.[2]
- Dealing with the constraints in resources (human, technical and financial) and respect legal framework.

Approach and intervention

In order to address the context and challenges described above OSIPTEL decided to make the best use of technologies to be more efficient and effective. This will allow OSIPTEL to save time, money and staff hours, which, in turn, can be used to address new issues and demands. In this order of ideas, OSIPTEL conducted last year an evaluation of all its processes and started to develop a technological tool for open data, entitled "PUNKU".

Concerning the process evaluation, on 2018 OSIPTEL mapped all processes (formal and informal), analysed their automation level and classified and prioritised them, creating clusters. In total, OSIPTEL mapped 128 processes: 43 strategic, 29 operative and 59 supporting processes. The first cluster to have been evaluated in depth is the one constituted by the following processes:

- inspection
- enforcement

- users' claims
- documentary procedures, being the processes that more expenses demand for the regulator.

Each process evaluation follows two steps: redesign and implementation.

OSIPTEL have already made some changes on the inspections and users´ claims process, approving last year the New Inspection Approach (Resolution No. 255-2018-CD/OSIPTEL) and starting with electronic notification. The New Inspection Approach searches to save time and money by changing the inspection technique: prioritising connectivity to telecommunication companies (in order to access to on-line information), focusing on three types of information:

- Monitoring of networks (to have information about quality, service interruptions).
- Claims on first instance.[3]
- Consumers services channels.

Electronic notification is cost efficient, considering that OSIPTEL has to notify more than 250 000 resolutions a year.

In addition, OSIPTEL has already prepared the terms of reference to hire a consultancy service to help with the redesign of all four process of the first cluster, mentioned above.

The consultants must compile information about the process, the main participants, the legal framework, the resources used, the information flow and their quantities, among others and identify main problems as well as propose possible solutions. These solutions must contemplate a process completely digitalised and the technological platforms needed to accomplish this goal. In addition, business intelligence associated with the process should be proposed.

The idea is to have on one side digital files (non-confidential documents) shared with regulated entities and/or users and the public and on the other side a platform to allow the exchange of information with the stakeholders. These exchanges could for instance concern administrative processes or statistics relating to these processes that could help decision making of senior management. For example, an automatic way to have data about which enterprises comply less with regulations, the levels of sanctions imposed in each case, the rules that the operators do not follow or the most popular claims, could serve to better decisions on regulations *ex post* evaluations and identifying gaps on current rules, as well as to measure our performance and the impact of our regulations.

Regarding open data, OSIPTEL is finalising the implementention of "PUNKU", an application that provides statistical information of the telecommunications sector in an interactive way and promote transparency. Information includes data concerning traffic, connections, lines, market share, financial numbers, and claims. Users will have access to general data but can also require reports and indicators (graphics and excel). Consequently, "PUNKU" will enable consumers, enterprises and government to take better informed decisions. Moreover, OSIPTEL will save time on processing data, making graphics and tables and even avoiding information requirements process, since everything will be available in "PUNKU".

The information that feeds PUNKU is collected quarterly, by semester o year. The operators send this information to OSIPTEL using SIGEP (an on-line system) and after some validations and consistency tests, non-confidential data is transfer to PUNKU to be available to the public. PUNKU is already in place at https://punku.osiptel.gob.pe/.

Results, impact and lessons learnt

The impacts of these changes are not yet entirely measurable, since most of them are still being implemented. Some positive outcomes are listed below.

Concerning the change in approach of the inspection process, (from field inspection to connectivity and in-house analysis), it has been estimated that OSIPTEL would save about 30% of the current budget allocated to its activity of network monitoring. Merely by avoiding trips and interactions with organisations to get information on quality of services, the savings in terms of staff hours must be underlined too, since the efforts to get the correct information (letters, meetings, etc.) are huge.

Savings resulting from "digital file" would also significant. Indeed an inspection file counts on average 105 pages and an enforcement file counts on average 30 pages. Companies usually request copies of all the files at least once during the process. The digital file would allow saving at least the shipping costs and the staff hours required to make copies, to prepare CDs/CDV with information, etc. In addition, having a platform will facilitate a fast exchange of information and promote transparency.

Regarding second instance claims, OSIPTEL had already started to notify electronically. Currently about 20% of the notifications are electronic and it could reach 80% by the end of the year. Considering that OSIPTEL notifies around 23 000 resolutions per month and that the average cost per notification is around USD 1.5, this change would represent more than USD 25 000 in savings per month (around USD 300 000 for a year), without considering staff hours saved. OSIPTEL believes that other improvements on the process could be made and that more technology should be used. This would allow OSIPTEL to reallocate resources to other activities.

Finally, thanks to "PUNKU", telecommunications market data will be accessible to a wide range of users, making consumers and operators' decisions more informed and efficient. The regulator will also take advantage of this information on all processes (regulation, inspection, and consumer's services) and senior executives will have interactive information readily available for decision making. In addition, we will avoid requirements of information (around 150 a year).

Notes

[1] It was created by the Legislative Decree No. 702 in 1991 and effectively starting operations in 1994.

[2] As stablished on OSIPTEL Strategic Plan 2018-2022, https://www.osiptel.gob.pe/categoria/plan-estrategico-institucional.

[3] OSIPTEL is in charge of user claims as second instance, but the majority of them are solved on first instance (more than 95%), meaning that we do not have details about 95% of the claims, information that can be valuable not only for inspection matters but for identify serious market problems.

The panorama of Portuguese water regulation: Case study on the Water and Waste Services Regulation Authority (ERSAR)

Context

Considering the evolution of the water sector over the last 25 years and given the absence of a clear national water strategy, it became urgent to globally reorganise the water sector. The reality was that a large number of municipalities of small and medium size provided poor quality of service in general, with no proper infrastructure, financial resources or skilled human resources and had difficulties to implement new European standards.

To implement this sector reorganisation, it was necessary to establish a new set of global, integrated and stable public policies, backed by a solid regulatory, legal and institutional framework, but also to define a territorial reorganisation of the services (promoting economies of scale), and new management models. These new governance tools allowed to further develop the water business sector, introduce competition with a focus on full-cost recovery, define service quality goals, improve drinking water quality, and finally promote the consumer protection and awareness.

Although great improvements occurred, this reorganisation process is still ongoing and there is still room for improvement.

The Water and Waste Services Regulation Authority *(Entidade Reguladora dos Serviços de Águas e Resíduos,* ERSAR) evolved accordingly but challenges remain because efficiency is increasingly becoming a paramount issue for adequate service provision, and further specialisation is required due to the changes occurred in the water sector.

Issues

The regulator's previous organisational structure was not able to cope with the current and future challenges posed by the changes in the sector. Indeed, the previous organisational structure was based on functional departments, namely two engineering departments (water and waste), a financial and economic regulation department, a legal department and a water quality department. Cross-functional and support departments included IT, finance and human resources, administrative and a strategic projects department focused on crosscutting projects.

Before the organisational reengineering, the major challenges were:

- Knowledge management: Poor specialised knowledge regarding how to interact with different governance models in a context where the regulatory processes differ for each management model.
- Process efficiency: Delays in responding to requests due to:
  - a lack of priority definition, planning and communication between different teams;
  - poor job descriptions, a lack of accountability and task delegation, diverting the focus for operational execution;

- o an unbalanced distribution of work among different professional groups (engineers, economists and legal staff), depending on the management model requirements.
- Service standardisation: A lack of "standardised services" provided by ERSAR, leading to:
  - o different outputs, depending on the issuer specialisation;
  - o different tariff analysis or investment plan analysis, depending on the analyst specialisation;
  - o different water quality characteristics, regardless of the regulated entities supporting management model.
- No segregation of duties between two incompatible regulatory roles: Regulation definition and regulated entities monitoring.

Approach and intervention

In that context, the need to rethink ERSAR's organisation and to convey a more agile and responsive service to regulated entities became necessary. The restructuring focused in three main pillars:

- Having focused teams, specialised in the specificities of each management model, leveraging know-how in similar processes and applicable legislation;
- Providing a single point of contact, aggregating the sector-specific knowledge with different academic backgrounds;
- Having focused team members, acquainted in the specific characteristics of each regulated entity, and able to follow its development.

From another perspective, the perception that regulators are data-driven organisations and that regulation is a data-driven activity, pose additional challenges to ERSAR. New technologies can introduce higher efficiency in the treatment of an increasing volume of data generated by regulated entities, but the use of these new tools also poses challenges to ERSAR and regulated entities, particularly:

- Decide upon the frequency of reports, such as Quality of Service, which is currently done once a year;
- Choose between different data upload mechanisms, which are still based on spreadsheets and that could be replaced by more direct and efficient procedures, based in interconnected information systems, enabling real-time reporting;
- Overcome obstacles related with the access to technology by regulated entities, since not all have the same expertise, financial and technological resources to deal with change;
- Engage with consumers using different sources of information, different platforms, channels and tools, from static internet websites to mobile user centric apps or even analytical powered tools;
- Finally, help regulated entities face Industry 4.0 and Technological disruption, which pose new needs for regulation, specifically, technological and cybersecurity regulation.

Identified key success factors for the change management process and the restructured organisation:

- Clearer duties and responsibilities, job descriptions, skills and competencies for each department;
- Assignment of a single focal point to each regulated entity, following agile, responsive and specialisation key factors, allowing to address three major challenges (service should be understood as the set of governance activities of defining, applying and monitoring regulatory activities):

- o from a service orientation perspective, the possibility for a regulated entity to interact with a single associated department
- o from a department perspective, the ability to address an end-to-end "service provision"
- o from a department perspective, the ability to define a regulatory strategy, implement it and monitor the result, in an overall "service lifecycle" perspective
- Process formalisation, procedure and activity identification, focusing on standardisation and best practice approaches, promoting continuous improvement and the usage of similar tools and methodologies among similar regulated entities and departments;
- Revision of internal and regulatory calendar time constraints, promoting a more balanced result in specific regulatory activities (e.g. rebalancing of concessional contracts);
- Regulatory information system optimisation, with:
  - o seamless integration of the different existing modules
  - o development and integration of new modules that support the overall regulatory activity, namely reengineered processes, focused in a collaborative approach
  - o data centralisation, following a data architecture model that supports the new agile organisation
  - o more agile and flexible data input processes from the regulated entities, promoting automatic interaction between IT systems, without neglecting the need to assure eventual information exclusion from less mature entities
  - o new analytical functionalities, using state of the art approaches (business intelligence/big data) but also new disruptive analytical technologies (machine learning and data science) and the skills and organisational structure that supports them.
- Overall performance management driven by quality.

Results, impact and lessons learnt

Although the process is not yet finished, the major outcomes can be summarised as:

Results

- One single department that aggregates the interactions with each regulated entity, resulting in bilateral synergy creation, and a closer relationship with the regulated entities, improving the knowledge about the regulated entities.
- A clearer intervention of each department in the regulatory process, enhancing human resources specialisation and knowledge management, higher process efficiency and standardised outputs, with an improved quality of service towards regulated entities.

Impacts

- An improved regulatory process management, focused on each management model lifecycle.
- A more agile and responsive organisation, capable of rapidly adapting the changes in the sector and to react to more disruptive management models.
- A higher satisfaction of the regulated entities regarding the regulator follow-up activities.
- However, it is not yet clear that process efficiency increased and that timely response improved, since:

- There are still information gaps between teams that undermine priority definition, planning and communication between different teams.
- Some issues remain in terms of job descriptions, lack of accountability and task delegation, increasing firefighting and diverting the focus from operational execution.
- A certain degree of unbalanced distribution of work among different professional groups still persists in some areas, depending on the management model requirements.

Lessons learnt and to be learned

- Change management process: A change management process must be in place. Motivational and resistance to change always inhibit the proper development of a move towards an AGILE organisation.
- Continuous process reengineering: It is always possible to further optimise processes. The organisational landscape changed and some tasks/activities are still performed manually, without the proper technological support, by the wrong person, or end up not being executed at all. To prevent this from happening an enterprise architecture approach is being used in order to cover more aspects of the new organisation design: processes, roles, job descriptions, technology and, most of all, business objects that circulate within personal computers, like spreadsheets, limiting the overall perspective of organisational behaviours and information flows, supporting processes and associated technology.
- Culture change: Culture has not yet completely changed. Some misconceptions about a process driven organisation and the ability to regulate in a more project driven AGILE approach persist. An AGILE project driven perspective could benefit the organisation. The power of a fully AGILE team is yet to be obtained.
- AGILE principles: AGILE organisational approaches imply less documentation and more technological collaboration. This is still hard to obtain due to old and lasting habits and the need to formalise all the interactions, leading to a new challenge: simplification and virtualisation of processes.
- Technological regulation: Ability to realise the need for new types of behavioural regulation: technological and cyber regulation, or structural regulation. The impact of new management models leveraged by disruptive technologies, e.g. the "Uberisation effect", with multi-sided business models and platforms on top of the existing service provisioning. The need to add extra regulation, considering the emergence of IoT (Internet of Things) technology, which enables the transfer of data over a network without requiring human-to-human or human-to-computer interaction. This brings improved operational efficiency but also new risks, not yet known by the sector, such as intrusion and hacking, denial of service, deconfiguration and loss of privacy with possible malfunctions and risks for the overall operation, directly affecting consumers and the regulated entities, with the power of destabilising the entire sector. Technological regulation is therefore increasingly important, with the need to regulate activities impacted by new disruptive technologies.